STATE VOTER REGISTRATION DATABASES

IMMEDIATE ACTIONS AND FUTURE IMPROVEMENTS

INTERIM REPORT

Committee on State Voter Registration Databases

Computer Science and Telecommunications Board

Division on Engineering and Physical Sciences

NATIONAL RESEARCH COUNCIL
OF THE NATIONAL ACADEMIES

THE NATIONAL ACADEMIES PRESS
Washington, D.C.
www.nap.edu

THE NATIONAL ACADEMIES PRESS   500 Fifth Street, NW   Washington, DC 20001

NOTICE: The project that is the subject of this report was approved by the Governing Board of the National Research Council, whose members are drawn from the councils of the National Academy of Sciences, the National Academy of Engineering, and the Institute of Medicine. The members of the committee responsible for the report were chosen for their special competences and with regard for appropriate balance.

This project was supported by Contract No. N01-OD-4-2139 between the National Academy of Sciences and the U.S. Election Assistance Commission. Any opinions, findings, conclusions, or recommendations expressed in this publication are those of the author(s) and do not necessarily reflect the view of the organizations or agencies that provided support for this project.

International Standard Book Number 13: 978-0-309-11878-1
International Standard Book Number 10: 0-309-11878-6

Copies of this report are available from

The National Academies Press
500 Fifth Street, NW
Box 285
Washington, DC 20055

800-624-6242
202-334-3313 (in the Washington metropolitan area)
http://www.nap.edu

Copyright 2008 by the National Academy of Sciences. All rights reserved.

Printed in the United States of America

THE NATIONAL ACADEMIES
Advisers to the Nation on Science, Engineering, and Medicine

The **National Academy of Sciences** is a private, nonprofit, self-perpetuating society of distinguished scholars engaged in scientific and engineering research, dedicated to the furtherance of science and technology and to their use for the general welfare. Upon the authority of the charter granted to it by the Congress in 1863, the Academy has a mandate that requires it to advise the federal government on scientific and technical matters. Dr. Ralph J. Cicerone is president of the National Academy of Sciences.

The **National Academy of Engineering** was established in 1964, under the charter of the National Academy of Sciences, as a parallel organization of outstanding engineers. It is autonomous in its administration and in the selection of its members, sharing with the National Academy of Sciences the responsibility for advising the federal government. The National Academy of Engineering also sponsors engineering programs aimed at meeting national needs, encourages education and research, and recognizes the superior achievements of engineers. Dr. Charles M. Vest is president of the National Academy of Engineering.

The **Institute of Medicine** was established in 1970 by the National Academy of Sciences to secure the services of eminent members of appropriate professions in the examination of policy matters pertaining to the health of the public. The Institute acts under the responsibility given to the National Academy of Sciences by its congressional charter to be an adviser to the federal government and, upon its own initiative, to identify issues of medical care, research, and education. Dr. Harvey V. Fineberg is president of the Institute of Medicine.

The **National Research Council** was organized by the National Academy of Sciences in 1916 to associate the broad community of science and technology with the Academy's purposes of furthering knowledge and advising the federal government. Functioning in accordance with general policies determined by the Academy, the Council has become the principal operating agency of both the National Academy of Sciences and the National Academy of Engineering in providing services to the government, the public, and the scientific and engineering communities. The Council is administered jointly by both Academies and the Institute of Medicine. Dr. Ralph J. Cicerone and Dr. Charles M. Vest are chair and vice chair, respectively, of the National Research Council.

www.national-academies.org

COMMITTEE ON STATE VOTER REGISTRATION DATABASES

FRANCES ULMER, University of Alaska, Anchorage, *Co-chair*
OLENE WALKER, State of Utah (retired), *Co-chair*
RAKESH AGRAWAL, Microsoft
R. MICHAEL ALVAREZ, California Institute of Technology
CHARLOTTE CLEARY, Independent Consultant
GARY W. COX, University of California, San Diego
PAULA HAWTHORN, Independent Consultant
SARAH BALL JOHNSON, Kentucky State Board of Elections
JEFF JONAS, IBM Corporation
JOHN LINDBACK, Office of the Secretary of State, Oregon
BRUCE McPHERSON, State of California (retired)
WENDY NOREN, Boone County Clerk's Office
WILLIAM WINKLER, U.S. Census Bureau
REBECCA N. WRIGHT, Rutgers University

SHARON PRIEST, Downtown Little Rock Partnership, resigned from the committee in December 2007

Staff

HERBERT S. LIN, Study Director
KRISTEN R. BATCH, Associate Program Officer
MORGAN R. MOTTO, Senior Program Assistant
BRANDYE WILLIAMS, Program Assistant

COMPUTER SCIENCE AND TELECOMMUNICATIONS BOARD

JOSEPH F. TRAUB, Columbia University, *Chair*
ERIC BENHAMOU, Benhamou Global Ventures, LLC
FREDERICK R. CHANG, University of Texas, Austin
WILLIAM DALLY, Stanford University
MARK E. DEAN, IBM Almaden Research Center
DEBORAH L. ESTRIN, University of California, Los Angeles
JOAN FEIGENBAUM, Yale University
KEVIN KAHN, Intel Corporation
JAMES KAJIYA, Microsoft Corporation
MICHAEL KATZ, New York University
RANDY KATZ, University of California, Berkeley
SARA KIESLER, Carnegie Mellon University
JON KLEINBERG, Cornell University
TERESA H. MENG, Stanford University
PRABHAKAR RAGHAVAN, Yahoo! Research
FRED B. SCHNEIDER, Cornell University
DAVID E. SHAW, D.E. Shaw & Co.
ALFRED Z. SPECTOR, Google, Inc.
WILLIAM STEAD, Vanderbilt University
ANDREW VITERBI, Viterbi Group, LLC
PETER WEINBERGER, Google, Inc.

Staff

JON EISENBERG, Director
KRISTEN R. BATCH, Associate Program Officer
RADHIKA CHARI, Administrative Coordinator
RENEE HAWKINS, Financial Associate
HERBERT S. LIN, Chief Scientist
MORGAN R. MOTTO, Senior Program Assistant
LYNETTE I. MILLETT, Senior Program Officer
DAVID PADGHAM, Associate Program Officer
JANICE M. SABUDA, Senior Program Assistant
TED SCHMITT, CSTB Consultant
BRANDYE WILLIAMS, Program Assistant
JOAN WINSTON, Program Officer

For more information on CSTB, see its Web site at http://www.cstb.org, write to CSTB, National Research Council, 500 Fifth Street, N.W., Washington, DC 20001, call (202) 334-2605, or e-mail the CSTB at cstb@nas.edu.

Preface

In late 2006, the National Research Council (NRC) convened the Committee on State Voter Registration Databases. Supported by the U.S. Election Assistance Commission, the committee was charged with organizing a series of workshops and the preparation of an interim report addressing challenges in implementing and maintaining state voter registration databases and providing advice to the states on how to evolve and maintain these databases in order to share information with other states securely and accurately in fulfillment of the Help America Vote Act of 2002. The committee's charge is laid out in Box P.1.

This report is an interim report to the Election Assistance Commission that outlines various challenges to the deployment of state voter registration databases and describes potential solutions to these challenges. Some of these solutions can be implemented prior to the November 2008 election; others will require a longer timeline for implementation and indeed some serious thought about how they might be implemented.

This study was undertaken by a committee of 14 people with a broad range of expertise and backgrounds, including election operations, databases, computer and network security, and political science (see Appendix F)—such a range was necessary to address the topic of state voter registration in all of its organizational, technical, and political complexity. To put information on the public record quickly and to educate the committee, two workshops were held in August and November 2007, the agendas for which are provided in Appendix E.

The committee has focused on shorter-term recommendations, both because that was what it was asked to do and because it had a limited time to develop an information-gathering record or to consider more complex, longer-term issues. However, on several issues the committee does provide a small number of long-range recommendations in this report. The committee's final report will elaborate on the argumentation underlying the long-range recommendations and on the recommendations themselves as needed—and in particular will address considerations related to interstate interoperability of voter registration databases.

The committee thanks those who participated in the first two workshops and contributed to the committee's deliberations (listed in Appendix E). It also extends special appreciation to Brad Bryant for coordinating the participation of election officials in these workshops and to the National Association of State Election Directors for being willing to share with the committee the results of its 2007 survey of state election officials regarding their voter registration databases. Finally, the committee thanks the NRC staff for their work on this report. Herb Lin provided invaluable and expert assistance to the committee by sorting through comments and suggestions and by drafting the report with the committee's guidance. Kristen Batch did a masterful job in organizing the workshops that served as the information basis for this report and in preparing the report for review. Jon Eisenberg, director of the Computer Science and Telecommunications Board, worked closely with the Election Assistance Commission to launch this study. Brandye Williams and Morgan Motto provided administrative support, and Radhika Chari provided overall administrative coordination.

Frances Ulmer and Olene Walker, *Co-chairs*
Committee on State Voter Registration Databases

> **BOX P.1**
> **Statement of Task**
>
> An ad hoc committee will organize a series of workshops and prepare an interim report addressing challenges in implementing and maintaining state voter registration databases and providing advice to the states on how to evolve and maintain these databases in order to share information with other states securely and accurately in fulfillment of the Help America Vote Act of 2002.
>
> A series of workshops will explore issues including the following:
>
> - Lessons learned from intrastate voter registration database interoperability efforts
> - Technical approaches, processes and safeguards associated with identifying and removing duplicate registrations
> - Technical approaches and procedures for sharing voter registration data across state systems
> - Security issues that arise when sharing data among states, and technical and procedural approaches for addressing them.
>
> Discussions at the workshops, expert testimony, and committee deliberations will be used to prepare an interim report outlining challenges to achieving interoperability of state voter registration databases and related challenges facing states as they develop, maintain, and evolve their voter registration databases. The interim report will also describe potential solutions to these challenges and discuss specific timelines over which state and local election officials could implement possible solutions, including solutions that could be implemented prior to the 2008 Federal election.
>
> Additional workshops and committee deliberations will culminate in a final report that builds on the interim report by describing technical, procedural, and organizational impediments to full voter registration database interoperability and outlining a plan for achieving interstate interoperability of state voter registration databases. The final report will address such issues as:
>
> - What is the current state of voter registration databases across the states?
> - What functionality is useful for a state in checking its voter registration database against that of another state?
> - What are the main technical, procedural, and organizational impediments standing in the way of full interoperability?
> - What paths to interstate interoperability minimize technical risk and expense?

Acknowledgment of Review Participants

This report has been reviewed in draft form by individuals chosen for their diverse perspectives and technical expertise, in accordance with procedures approved by the National Research Council's Report Review Committee. The purpose of this independent review is to provide candid and critical comments that will assist the institution in making its published report as sound as possible and to ensure that the report meets institutional standards for objectivity, evidence, and responsiveness to the study charge. The review comments and draft manuscript remain confidential to protect the integrity of the deliberative process. We wish to thank the following individuals for their review of this report:

Elwyn R. Berlekamp, University of California, Berkeley,
Brad Bryant, Kansas Secretary of State Office,
Alan H. Davidson, Election Management Solutions, Inc.,
Morris P. Fiorina, Jr., Stanford University,
Venkatesh Ganti, Microsoft Research,
Lloyd J. Leonard, League of Women Voters of the United States,
Deirdre K. Mulligan, University of California, Berkeley,
Glenn Newkirk, InfoSENTRY Services, Inc., and
Daniel P. Tokaji, Ohio State University.

Although the reviewers listed above have provided many constructive comments and suggestions, they were not asked to endorse the conclusions or recommendations, nor did they see the final draft of the report before its release. The review of this report was overseen by Elsa M. Garmire, Dartmouth College. Appointed by the National Research Council, she was responsible for making certain that an independent examination of this report was carried out in accordance with institutional procedures and that all review comments were carefully considered. Responsibility for the final content of this report rests entirely with the authoring committee and the institution.

Contents

SYNOPSIS 1

INTERIM REPORT 4

    The Context for Voter Registration, 4
    Key Processes for Voter Registration Databases, 4
    Technical Considerations for Voter Registration Databases, 8
    Immediate Actions Possible Before November 2008, 10
    Possible Future Improvements That Will Require Longer-Term Action, 15

APPENDIXES

A	Background and Context	23
B	Matching Records Across Databases	29
C	Data Issues	41
D	Security and Privacy	48
E	Workshop Agendas	53
F	Biographical Information	58

Synopsis

Voter registration plays a central role in elections in all states except North Dakota. Today, the states operate under a federal mandate (the Help America Vote Act (HAVA) of 2002) to develop "a single, uniform, official, centralized, interactive computerized statewide voter registration list defined, maintained, and administered at the state level."[1] Each state's database must contain the name and registration information of each legally registered voter in the state, and each legally registered voter is assigned a unique identifier. Election officials must perform regular maintenance regarding the accuracy of the registration lists. In addition, the National Voter Registration Act (NVRA) of 1993 and HAVA establish rules under which names may be removed from voter registration lists. (A voter registration list is the list of names contained in a voter registration database, and the terms are often used interchangeably.)

Two basic tasks must be performed for voter registration databases: adding individuals to the voter registration database (VRD) and maintaining the VRD.

- Adding individuals to the VRD generally requires that the information provided on a first-time voter registration application be verified against the relevant state's department of motor vehicles database of driver's license numbers or the Social Security Administration's database of Social Security numbers.
- Maintaining the VRD is needed to keep voter registration information current and to remove the names of ineligible voters and duplicate registrations from the voter lists. This task requires comparing records within a VRD to other records in order to identify duplicate registrations (usually associated with changes of address or name) and (by law) comparing VRDs to databases of known felons, deceased individuals, and individuals declared mentally incompetent. In addition, address changes for drivers' licenses play a major role in updating and maintaining the VRD.

Both of these tasks require databases that are accurate and complete, as well as good matching procedures. However, in practice, a variety of practical problems arise such as data entry error. In addition, the matching procedures used by many states have not been subjected to rigorous evaluation or testing.

The VRD also drives the preparation of pollbooks (the list of eligible voters in localities for use at polling places). Additional functionality implemented by many states in their (centralized) voter registration systems—including ballot preparation; signature verification for absentee or mail-in ballots; and management of election workers, polling places, petitions, and requirements for disability access under HAVA—assists the local elections official in conducting an election.

Given the time frame needed to implement changes that require the modification of computer systems (which involve at a minimum time to design, code, and test changes, and may require new procurements and/or procedures), it is unlikely that any recommendation concerning technology changes could be responsibly implemented in time for the 2008 elections. Moreover, solutions to these technical problems may in some cases also require changes to state election law and/or regulation; they are not

---

[1] Section 303(a)(1)(A) of HAVA.

exclusively issues about changing computer systems, but also might require that states alter law, regulation, or practice.

Nevertheless, the Committee on State Voter Registration Databases believes that a number of meaningful changes of a nontechnical nature can be implemented in two areas in time to make a difference in the November 2008 election: (1) education and dissemination of information and (2) administrative processes and procedures. In addition, this interim report notes a number of actions that can be taken to support elections in 2010 and beyond, although states may wish to examine these longer-term actions to see if any can be implemented in the few months before the 2008 election.

These short-term changes and longer-term actions are directed primarily at election officials (voter registrars) at the state and local/county level. In some cases, the Election Assistance Commission has a useful role to play as well in facilitating and promoting their implementation.

SHORT-TERM ACTIONS—PUBLIC EDUCATION AND DISSEMINATION OF INFORMATION

- Raise public awareness about the legibility and the completeness of voter registration card information. Jurisdictions could take some or all of the following specific steps:

  —Emphasize in the instructions for filling out voter registration forms the importance of legibility and completeness (for example, "Please print all responses; if your answers are illegible, your application may be mis-entered, rejected, or returned to you.").
  —Conduct media campaigns emphasizing the importance of legibility and completeness in the information provided on voter registration forms.
  —Coordinate with third-party voter registration groups and public service agencies, emphasizing the need for their field volunteers to attend to legibility and completeness as they distribute and/or collect registration materials.

SHORT-TERM ACTIONS—ADMINISTRATIVE PROCESSES AND PROCEDURES

- Resubmit match queries if the response returned from the Social Security Administration or department of motor vehicles is a nonmatch.
- Provide human review of all computer-indicated removal decisions.
- Improve the transparency of procedures for adding voters and for list maintenance.
- Use fill-in online registration forms.
- Perform empirical testing on the adequacy of processes for adding to and maintenance of lists.
- Take steps to minimize errors during data entry.
- Allow selected individuals to suppress address information on public disclosures of voter registration status.
- Encourage (but do not require) entities sponsoring voter registration drives to submit voter registration forms in a timely manner to reduce massive influxes at the registration deadline.

LONG-TERM ACTIONS FOR POSSIBLE FUTURE IMPROVEMENTS

- Develop and promote public access portals for online checking of voter registration status.
- Encourage/require departments of motor vehicles as well as public assistance and disability service agencies to provide voter registration information electronically.
- Encourage/require departments of motor vehicles, public assistance and disability service agencies, tax assessors, and other public service agencies of state and local government in their communications with the public to remind voters to check and update their information.
- Improve matching procedures.
- Establish a software repository of tested matching algorithms.
- Provide voter registration receipts to improve administrative processes.
- Allow voters to register and to update missing or incorrect registration information online if a signature is already on file with a state agency.
- Develop procedures for handling disenfranchisement caused by mistaken removals from voter registration lists.
- Improve the design of voter registration forms.

Interim Report

THE CONTEXT FOR VOTER REGISTRATION

Voter registration plays a central role in elections in most states. Today, every state except North Dakota[1] operates under a federal mandate (the Help America Vote Act (HAVA) of 2002) to develop "a single, uniform, official, centralized, interactive computerized statewide voter registration list defined, maintained, and administered at the state level."[2] Each state's database must contain the name and registration information of each legally registered voter in the state, and each legally registered voter is assigned a unique identifier. Election officials must perform regular maintenance regarding the accuracy and completeness of the registration lists. In addition, the National Voter Registration Act (NVRA) of 1993 and HAVA establish rules under which names may be removed from voter registration lists.

As a registration deadline nears, the processing of voter registration applications can present enormous logistical problems. The reason is the sheer volume of voter registration records that need processing (either new voter registration applications or updates of information for already-registered voters)—and especially in a presidential election year, this volume can be a substantial fraction of the entire voter registration database. Most of these documents typically arrive within a few weeks of a registration deadline and, depending on the registration cutoff in a particular state, can mean around-the-clock data entry up to the last minute (that is, on Election Day) so that pollbooks can be printed. In some instances, there have been outstanding documents to be processed even by Election Day, and staff were needed to manage inquiries from polling places from a manual file of registration cards not yet entered.

A more detailed discussion of the background and context for voter registration can be found in Appendix A.

KEY PROCESSES FOR VOTER REGISTRATION DATABASES

It is helpful to consider the two basic information management functions of any voter registration database (VRD): adding individuals to the list and maintaining the list.[3] The VRD also drives the preparation of pollbooks (the list of eligible voters in localities for use at polling places). Many states have implemented additional functionality to their (centralized) voter registration systems that assists the local elections official in conducting an election. Such functionality may include ballot preparation, signature verification for absentee or mail-in ballots, management of election workers, polling places, petitions, and requirements for disability access under HAVA.

---

[1] North Dakota does not require voter registration and was exempted from certain provisions of HAVA. For more background information, see http://www.nd.gov/sos/forms/pdf/votereg.pdf.
[2] Section 303(a)(1)(A) of HAVA.
[3] These two general processes—verifying voter registration information and maintaining voter registration lists—are central to the technical and policy dimensions of voter registration databases. Other processes, not covered in this report, are relevant to other requirements and verification procedures covered under Section 303(b) of HAVA.

Posting New Voter Registration Information to a Voter Registration Database

In processing a voter registration application form, the first question is whether the applicant is already on the list (e.g., the person may already be on the list but with a different address, or the person may have changed his or her name due to a marriage, divorce, or legal action). Although states handle this process in different ways, one notional way of handling it is that if the person is already in the VRD, the status of the previous registration is changed to "out-of-date" and a pointer added to the new registration. The new registration information must then be added to the VRD, just as it must be if the new registrant is not on the list, except that the verification procedures described below are then not relevant. Alternatively, the database's functionality may allow an update of the voter's registration to reflect the new information regarding address or name.

In those instances in which data are entered in a distributed manner throughout the state, checking to see if the applicant is already in the VRD may occur after the applicant has been added as a new registrant. In this case, the new record must be handled as a duplicate of an existing record, each referring to the same person but with different recorded information.

If the registrant is not already in the state's VRD, the individual must be considered a first-time applicant. (In addition, some states regard a voter as a "new registration" when he or she moves from one jurisdiction to another within the state—even if the voter is contained in the statewide VRD, the registration is valid only in the first jurisdiction.) HAVA requires certain procedures for verifying voter registration applications. With some exceptions,[4] first-time applicants are required to provide a current and valid driver's license number (or a state-issued nondriver's identification) or, lacking one, the last four digits of their Social Security number (SSN).[5] Those who register by mail are also required to present identifying information at the polls on Election Day (or with their mail-in ballots if they vote via mail) if their department of motor vehicles (DMV) or Social Security Administration (SSA) information cannot be verified. HAVA requires the state motor vehicle agencies and the SSA to enter into agreements with states to verify voter registration information. Currently, the American Association of Motor Vehicle Administrators and the Social Security Administration are using the first name, last name, month and year of birth, and last four digits of the SSN (SSN4) for the verification process.

Under these agreements, the applicant's information can be verified against the information on file with the DMV or the SSA. In the case of a nonmatch (for example, the applicant cannot be found in the DMV or SSA databases), HAVA and other relevant federal laws provide little guidance or direction to the states about what to do next (with one exception[6]). Although in most states the voter registrar will make an attempt to contact the applicant so that he or she can provide additional information, there is variation in how the states manage the nonmatch, some of which is the subject of current legal challenges.[7]

---

[4] See HAVA Section 303(b) for the exceptions for individuals who register or vote by mail, are entitled to vote by absentee ballot under the Uniformed and Overseas Citizens Absentee Voting Act, or are provided the right to vote under the Voting Accessibility for the Elderly and Handicapped Act.

[5] If the applicant has neither a driver's license nor an SSN, the jurisdiction is required to provide the applicant with a unique voter identifying number.

[6] See HAVA Section 303(b). In the event that an individual registers to vote by mail without providing a copy of a current and valid driver's license or other appropriate form of identification with the application, and his or her information cannot be verified (matched) against the DMV or SSA databases, HAVA requires this individual to present appropriate identification at the polling place on Election Day.

[7] For example, in a case being litigated as this report is written, a Washington state law is being challenged that requires a nonmatch to result in an applicant not being registered. See *Washington Association of Churches v. Reed*, No. C06-0726RSM, 2006 WL 4604854, available at http://projectvote.org/fileadmin/ProjectVote/Legal_Documents/WAC_PI_Decision.pdf.

List Maintenance

A second important function of a VRD system is to maintain the list of eligible voters, that is, to keep voter registration information current and to remove the names of ineligible voters and duplicate registrations from the voter lists. Jurisdictions must perform periodic list maintenance in accordance with provisions of the NVRA.[8] Section 8 of the NVRA requires states to conduct a "general program that makes a reasonable effort to remove the names of ineligible voters" at voter request or as a result of a felony conviction (presuming that state law directs removal of felons from voter registration lists), mental incompetence, death, or change of residence outside the jurisdiction that holds the voter's registration. The NVRA requires that any program of systematic removal of names of ineligible voters must be completed not less than 90 days prior to a federal election. This time limit does not apply to removals due to death, felony conviction, or judgment of mental incompetence, which may occur within 90 days of an election. Neither HAVA nor the NVRA requires advance notification of removal from the registration list except in the case of change of residence outside the previous jurisdiction.

Felony Convictions, Death, and Mental Incompetence

HAVA calls for coordination of state VRDs with state death and felony databases in accordance with state law. The Election Assistance Commission (EAC) recommends that states also coordinate with relevant federal databases, Social Security Death Index databases, and criminal conviction records from U.S. attorneys and federal courts. The use of multiple databases is helpful to overcome gaps in or omissions of data from external state files.[9] However, HAVA does not specify how the coordination with other state agencies' databases is to take place and lacks specific guidance on standards or methods for removal of ineligible voters from the databases for these reasons.

Note also that state law governs state policy regarding the relationship between voting eligibility and status as a felon. In some states, convicted felons are never permitted to vote after their conviction; in other states, the right to vote is reinstated automatically upon the end of the individual's sentence; in still other states, the individual must apply for reinstatement after the end of his or her sentence or at a state-specified time afterward.

Changes of Residence

The NVRA requires states to establish a program to use information supplied by the U.S. Postal Service (USPS) to identify registrants whose address may have changed; today, about 14 percent of the population changes an address every year.[10] Identifying voters who have moved is usually based on periodic mailings that registrars send to all voters in the jurisdiction by U.S. mail, indicating on the envelope "do not forward but rather return to sender." Notices that are returned to the registrar are an indication that the voter may have moved.

The USPS does not automatically notify voter registrars of an individual's change of address. To use the USPS to check an individual's status, the voter registrar must initiate a query to the USPS with a

---

[8] See 42 U.S.C. 1973gg et seq., including Subsections (a)(4), (c)(2), (d), and (e) of Section 8 of that act (42 U.S.C. 1973gg-6).

[9] For instance, if a resident of Missouri dies in California, the death is recorded in California and notification may or may not be sent to Missouri in a timely manner, or ever.

[10] See U.S. Census Bureau, *Geographical Mobility*: 2006. Highlights from this series are available at http://www.census.gov/Press-Release/www/releases/archives/mobility_of_the_population/010755.html, and detailed tables are available at http://www.census.gov/population/www/socdemo/migrate.html.

list of names to see if anyone on the list has moved or submitted a change-of-address form. If so, the USPS will return to the voter registrar the new address for the relevant individuals if the query is made within the forwarding period. Queries made after that point indicate that the new address is unavailable. In addition, a voter registrar could, in principle, also check the entire VRD against the USPS National Change of Address (NCOA) database[11] to catch any additional missed moves,[12] although the actual utility and practicality of such a check may vary depending on the jurisdiction involved.

The NVRA requires election officials to notify the voter if they receive an indication that the voter has moved. In particular, when a change of address is received from the USPS process, the registrar must send a confirmation card to the voter. If the voter remains within the jurisdiction of the registrar, no further action is needed. However, if the new address is outside the jurisdiction of the registrar, the voter is asked to return the card, and the voter registration record is handled accordingly. If the confirmation card is not returned and the voter does not vote in or by the second general federal election that occurs after the date of the notice, he or she may be removed from the VRD.

Some states have implemented what is referred to as "portable" registration, meaning that registered voters who move within the state need not re-apply for registration at their new address; instead, procedures exist to automatically remove the voters from the registry at their old address and add them at their new address. In principle, such systems can mitigate problems arising from the single largest source of duplicate registrations that a state faces.

In addition, a state's department of motor vehicles can be an important (and in some cases is the primary) source of information regarding changes of address. States that have integrated their voter registration systems with DMV systems have found that many changes of address are much more easily managed.

Duplicate Registrations

Duplicate registrations in a VRD often cause confusion. For example, since voter turnout percentages are calculated on the basis of the actual number of voters on Election Day divided by the number of registered voters, a VRD with a large number of duplicate registrations can lead to underestimates of voter turnout. The same phenomenon has operational significance in states where referendum propositions require a certain percentage of registered voters to approve the placement of any given proposition on the ballot.

It is important to distinguish between two types of "duplicate" registrations. One type of duplicate (call it "Type A") is a record in a database that is identical in all particulars to another record—this may occur, for example, if an individual has submitted more than one registration application, as he or she may do entirely by accident if a previous registration is forgotten. In general, removing Type A duplicates from voter registration lists is technically easy to do.

A second type of duplicate (call it "Type B") is present when two records in the VRD with non-identical information correspond to the same individual. Type B duplicate registrations arise in many ways. Perhaps the most common source is a voter's change of address (for example, as the result of a move); a second common source is change of name (for example, as the result of marriage).

The NVRA establishes procedures that must be followed before a Type B duplicate registration is removed due to a change of address (though not for other reasons), and HAVA establishes a requirement that states provide a unique identifier for every registered voter that is intended to facilitate handling of

---

[11] For more information on the NCOA database and address change services provided by the U.S. Postal Service, see http://www.usps.com/ncsc/addressservices/moveupdate/changeaddress.htm.
[12] Commercial software costing in the range of $50,000 is available that checks addresses and formats them so that they can be checked against the NCOA. A less expensive option available to states is to contract with a vendor licensed by the USPS, which can cost several thousand dollars per year to check the entire state database.

Type B duplicates. The EAC's *Voluntary Guidance on Implementation of Statewide Voter Registration Lists* further states that "if a state has identified a name on the voter list that it believes is either a duplicate name (or an ineligible voter), election officials should contact the individual."[13] Nevertheless, states establish the technical criteria for deciding when a Type B duplicate exists and process removals according to their own state-specific rules and guidelines.

The best computer matching procedures that have been developed and compared by industry and academic researchers do not appear to be widely used by the states for voter registration purposes. Several of the procedures are relatively easy to implement and have been demonstrated to improve significantly on unsophisticated procedures. States that are not using these procedures can consider how to implement them and how to evaluate the effects of their implementations in reducing error rates.

Note also that the use of a unique identifier reduces the technical complexity of managing Type B duplicates. Nevertheless, some matching issues arise even if unique identifiers are present (for example, what to do in the event that the unique identifier is recorded incorrectly).

TECHNICAL CONSIDERATIONS FOR VOTER REGISTRATION DATABASES

A variety of technical issues affect the performance of voter registration databases. These issues and some of the areas for improvement are discussed below.

Data Capture and Quality

As is the case with all other databases, the utility of a VRD depends strongly on the quality of the data it contains, although a variety of processes can be applied to the data in order to improve their quality.

One common source of error in the data is data entry. Applicants typically submit handwritten voter registration cards that are sent to the voter registrar. The applicant can make a mistake, forget to answer a question, or not write legibly. The form or its information could be altered in transmission (a field could get smudged in postal handling, for example). Keying errors result in mistranscriptions.

Another source of error is the quality of other lists that are compared with VRDs. The quality of other lists similarly depends on the procedures for data collection and entry; methods employed to minimize errors in the data, such as removing duplicates and other anomalies from these secondary databases; and training provided to staff and monitoring of staff when entering data, among other aspects.

Moreover, the different purposes for which secondary data are collected can limit their use for other purposes and may not fully address what is needed for the purposes of voter registration databases. For instance, the USPS compiles change-of-address data when customers move and request forwarding services through the USPS National Change of Address system. However, because of privacy considerations the USPS limits the disclosure of this information. Also, USPS has defined its information services so as to serve its primary business function, that is, without considering the needs of voter registrars. As a result, the NCOA system cannot be queried with name and date of birth to find out where an individual has moved to; rather a name and address must be presented before the information can be validated.

The data contained in a VRD can be characterized with respect to two different attributes—accuracy and completeness. For purposes of this report, accuracy refers to the factual correctness of the data that exist in the database, whereas completeness refers to the presence in the database of all individuals who *should* be in the database. If the database is perfect, it is both 100 percent accurate and 100 percent complete—that is, all of the data in the database are correct (and thus the database contains

---

[13]See http://www.eac.gov/election/docs/statewide_registration_guidelines_072605.pdf/attachment_download/ file.

no individual who should not be in the database), *and* the database includes all of the individuals who should be in the database. Notice that in this formulation, accuracy does *not* subsume completeness, so that a database must be characterized with respect to *both* attributes.

This usage of the term "accurate" appears to be consistent with the meaning of the word in common discourse. However, the reader is cautioned that some other commentators and analysts use the term "accurate" to mean both "factually correct" and "complete."

Although accuracy and completeness are conceptually distinct attributes, they are generally linked, as the discussion in the next section on matching shows.

A more detailed discussion of data capture and quality can be found in Appendix C.

Matching

Adding new voters to the VRD and maintaining the VRD both require a procedure by which attributes of one data record (for example, a record of an individual in the VRD) are compared to attributes of another record (for example, a voter registration application, a DMV driver's license, an SSA record, a record in a database of felons, and so on). This procedure, variously known as record linkage, identity matching, identity resolution, or simply "record matching," is "good" when it results in low rates of false positives (matches indicated when no match in fact exists) and false negatives (nonmatches indicated when a match does in fact exist).

- In adding individuals to a VRD, poor procedures could result in improper indications of a nonmatch when a match should be indicated (a result that could be used to disenfranchise voters if an applicant's information cannot be verified or to inflate the size of the VRD list if an earlier registration for an applicant cannot be found) and/or improper indications of a match when a nonmatch should be indicated (a result that could be used to add ineligible names to the VRD list).
- In maintaining the VRD, procedures of poor quality will result in improper indications of a match between the voter registration list and one of the databases of ineligible-to-vote individuals when a nonmatch should be indicated (a result that tends to remove voters from the voter registration list improperly) or improper indications of a nonmatch when a match should be indicated (a result that would keep felons, mentally incompetent individuals, and deceased people in the VRD).

The consequences of false positives and false negatives may vary depending on the purpose of the matching (and thus depending on the other databases against which VRD records are being matched). By law, the information on new voter registration applications must be matched against DMV or SSA records, and the consequences of a false negative (that is, no matches found when an individual is in fact represented in the DMV or SSA database) may be to wrongly keep the individual off the rolls—false negatives in this context may lead to a less *complete* VRD. List maintenance often calls for existing VRD records to be matched against felon or death records. The consequences of a false negative are precisely the opposite: individuals may erroneously be kept on the rolls—false negatives in this context may lead to a less *accurate* VRD. The converse is true with respect to false positives.

Because of data quality issues and the lack of a truly unique identifier, record matching cannot be done perfectly in this context, that is, with zero false positives and zero false negatives. The consequence is that achieving the goal of a simultaneously 100 percent accurate and 100 percent complete voter registration list is virtually impossible. At the same time, what counts as an acceptable rate of false positives or false negatives, or an acceptable tradeoff between accuracy and completeness, depends on the particular policy goals that are desired.

For example, given that a choice is necessary, a state may prefer to emphasize completeness over accuracy in its VRD. With this goal in mind, it may choose to minimize the rate of false positives in matching the VRD against a list of felons, a policy choice that almost certainly will increase the number of ineligible individuals on the list. Alternatively, a state may prefer to emphasize accuracy over completeness in its VRD. With this goal in mind, it may choose to minimize the rate of false negatives in matching the VRD against a list of felons, a policy choice that almost certainly will increase the number of legitimately eligible individuals removed from the list.[14]

Note also that record-matching procedures can, in principle, be executed by computer, by a human being, or both. Computer-based procedures for verification or maintenance have the advantages that they can perform matches very rapidly and can operate consistently (because they depend only on the specific data involved and the prescriptive rules as implemented). But computers using naïve matching rules can also be "fooled" by data problems that suitably trained humans can often handle.

Human-based matching has the advantage of bringing to bear training and personal experience, which can be used to determine a match or nonmatch in any given case. However, human-based matching is impractical when large numbers of records are involved. Human-based matching is generally less consistent than computer-based matching but may be better in other areas, such as comparing signatures.

These procedures can be used in tandem, so that any anomaly found by a computer-based procedure is directed to a human being before any action is taken.[15] (In effect, however, these procedures can break down under the stress of large numbers of applications, as may happen when applications are submitted near the deadline for submission of registrations.)

A more detailed discussion of matching can be found in Appendix B. Some privacy issues that arise with matching are addressed in Appendix D.

IMMEDIATE ACTIONS POSSIBLE BEFORE NOVEMBER 2008

Given the time frame needed to implement changes that require the modification of computer systems (which involve at a minimum time to design, code, test, and document changes, and may require new procurements, procedures, and/or training), it is unlikely that any recommendation concerning technology changes could be responsibly implemented in time for the 2008 elections—indeed, if any state is planning significant technology changes intended for use in the 2008 elections, the committee recommends extreme caution in proceeding at this time.

This point does not mean that nothing can be done to improve the voter registration process between now and November 2008—the committee believes that a number of meaningful nontechnical changes can be implemented in time to make a difference. These changes are clustered in two areas: (1) education and dissemination of information and (2) administrative processes and procedures. Of course, implementation will depend on the availability of financial resources to support hitherto unanticipated

---

[14]Arguments might sometimes be put forth to make only a particular subset of the database maximally accurate or maximally complete. While legitimate policy reasons for doing so in some cases cannot be ruled out, such actions are inherently suspect and deserve the highest scrutiny before being implemented. For example, an election official might be motivated to maximize the number of voters in a particular socioeconomic class or other group in order to give his or her party of preference an advantage at the polls. Although the political motivation for wishing to take such action is clear, such an action would do serious injustice to the democratic process, and such a motivation would never be acknowledged publicly.

[15]These comments should not be taken to imply that the combination of computer plus human review is necessarily better than the computer alone in all circumstances. Indeed, the literature indicates that for human review to add to the quality of the outcome, human reviewers must be well trained (see, for example, H.B. Newcombe et al., "Reliability of Computerized Versus Manual Death Searches in a Study of the Health of Eldorado Uranium Workers," *Computers in Biology and Medicine* 13(3):157-69, 1983). Nonetheless, it tends to be true that the combination of good computer matching procedures and well-trained human reviewers is often superior in performance to the use of those procedures alone.

actions and activities—such resources are especially important when human-intensive actions are involved. The section "Possible Future Improvements That Will Require Longer-Term Action" identifies actions that can be taken to support elections in 2010 and beyond, although states may wish to examine these longer-term actions to see if any can be implemented in the few months before the 2008 election.

These short-term changes and longer-term actions are directed primarily at election officials (voter registrars) at the state and local/county level. In some cases, the Election Assistance Commission has a useful role to play as well in facilitating and promoting their implementation.

Public Education and Dissemination of Information

Raise Public Awareness About the Legibility and the Completeness of Voter Registration Card Information

Accurate and complete data are a basic element of a high-quality VRD. But as noted in Appendix C, the quality of the data in a VRD is no better than the data that are entered into the system. For example, illegible information impairs the ability of registrars to verify registrations as required by HAVA and/or state law, possibly placing additional downstream burdens on the voter (such as having to verify information by mail or having to provide an ID when voting the first time).

Efforts to raise public awareness about the importance of legibility and fully completing voter registration forms would help to reduce the amount of illegible or missing information on these forms when they are submitted for data entry. Properly undertaken, these efforts to raise public awareness of this particular issue could be integrated with ongoing efforts to encourage people to register to vote. Jurisdictions could take some or all of the following specific steps:

- Emphasize in the instructions for filling out voter registration forms the importance of legibility and completeness (for example, "Please print all responses; if your answers are illegible, your application may be mis-entered, rejected, or returned to you.").[16]
- Conduct media campaigns (perhaps undertaken by the Ad Council) emphasizing the importance of legibility and completeness in the information provided on voter registration forms.
- Coordinate with third-party voter registration groups and public service agencies, emphasizing the need for their field volunteers to attend to legibility and completeness as they distribute and/or collect registration materials.

Administrative Processes and Procedures

A variety of recommended administrative processes and procedures will also help to ensure higher-quality matching and increase voter confidence in VRDs. Note, however, that large volumes of registration forms usually need to be processed as registration deadlines approach, a workload for which jurisdictions commonly rely on temporary staff. Unless other arrangements are made to adjust workflow (such as ensuring that actions that require human judgment are routed to permanent staff), these temporary staff will, in many cases, have to carry out these recommended processes and procedures, suggesting that training them to do so will be necessary.

---

[16] Even the National Mail Voter Registration Form does not address this point.

Resubmit Match Queries If the Response Returned from the Social Security Administration or Department of Motor Vehicles Is a Nonmatch

An election official can use any additional information available to generate match variations for a given name. For example, a match might be sought on standard name variations (for example, Bill versus William), or transposed fields (for example, last name and first name), or compound names separated, or on a maiden name if available. Finally, it may be possible to resolve a nonmatch result by direct contact with the voter, either by phone or in writing.

Provide Human Review of All Computer-indicated Removal Decisions

Because inaccuracies in data may lead to false matching by automated processes, the committee urges jurisdictions to provide a human review of each and every decision to remove a registered voter from a VRD subject to the availability of trained personnel to do so. (Note that most of the parties responding to a 2007 survey of the National Association of State Election Directors on voter registration practices indicated that they did rely on humans to verify a match before a voter registration is canceled.[17])

For example, in one county, letters are sent to individuals who are at risk for being removed from the voter registration list; these letters have a "respond by date X or be deleted" notice. If a notice comes back as "undeliverable as addressed," the name of the individual is deleted after date X. If the issue is duplicate records (that is, if two records appear for the same individual), the incorrect record is deleted. To determine which record is correct, the county checks all data sources (for example, tax records, real estate records, and occasionally the telephone book) and/or contacts the voter.

Improve the Transparency of Procedures for Adding Voters and for List Maintenance

As noted in Appendix B, there is little transparency in the procedures of any given state for adding voters to a VRD or in maintaining the VRD itself. To improve transparency, the states and local jurisdictions if necessary would be well advised to:

- Develop written procedures for the verification of new voters and the handling of removals. These procedures should address explicitly the specific field-level and record-level matching criteria used for each of these processes. Written procedures are needed both to inform the public of what election officials intend to be done and to provide a standard for accountability regarding what is being done.
- Publicize these procedures widely.
- Collect and publish data on the outcomes of initial applications for registration:[18] How many applications were received? Of these, how many were approved and how many rejected? Of those rejected, what were the reasons for rejection—illegibility, incompleteness, person ineligible (cite reason for ineligibility), and so on.
- Collect and publish data on how the state handles removals from the registry: How many removals were made? Of these, how many were due to intrastate movement, death, and so on.

---

[17] See http://www.surveymonkey.com/sr.aspx?sm=jK8QyNXCIwgdaY4SjASFyN0v4coilbBEvQxDuSyIS4s_3d.
[18] Many jurisdictions already collect such data, and aggregations of some of these data are published in the EAC Election Day Survey. For more information on the Election Day Survey, see http://www.eac.gov/schedule/2008-election-day-survey/.

> **BOX I.1**
> **Examples of Auditing Applied to VRD Processes**
>
> *Auditing Removals from Voter Registration Rolls*
>
> Voter registrars need the date of receipt of registration applications, the date on which a registration-related notice was sent to the voter, the date, if any, of any response from the voter, and the date on which the corrected or completed information was received; indexes of all of these dates must be kept if correspondence and documentation are to be located. In one state, the denial letter is kept with the original application, and these are sorted by year of first receipt and then alphabetically by name. In this state's experience, the individuals claiming they had registered but not been found on the voter registration list had often received a copy of the removal letter, as could be demonstrated by referring to the voter's file.
>
> *Auditing Changes in Voter Registrations Records*
>
> The main text of this report suggests that voter access to a voter registration database (VRD) should be implemented through buffered access to a synchronized copy of the VRD, not to the VRD itself. One kind of audit procedure checks expected behavior against actual behavior. For example, an audit procedure could keep a log of which records were changed in the primary source (the VRD) since the last synchronization. This log could be used to identify the records in the copy that are supposed to be changed—changes in the copy that don't match this list would indicate a problem that election officials could and should investigate further.

- Audit the processes to ensure that procedures are being followed (see Box I.1 for examples).

Note that collecting and publishing the data suggested above can provide a basis for assessing how big a problem illegibility actually is, how many persons apply who are actually ineligible (for various reasons), and so on. The more of such data there are, the easier it will be for election officials to identify problems and to improve list maintenance procedures.

Use Fill-in Online Registration Forms

Typewritten or printed information is almost always more legible than handwritten information. Assuming they already have Web sites from which voters may obtain voter registration forms and other election-related materials, jurisdictions could encourage the use of fill-in online registration forms, such as fill-in PDF or Web forms that accept keyboard input (that can be printed, input and all); a number of states provide this service today. Although the form must still be printed, signed, and then mailed or delivered to the voter registrar, the information on the form will be much more legible. (Note that although the deployment of a new encoding of an old form—such as the National Mail Voter Registration Form—should be possible in a relatively short time frame (the EAC is a logical focal point for any such effort), it should not be regarded as a trivial effort that can be accomplished without some care and testing.)

Perform Empirical Testing on the Adequacy of Processes for Adding to and Maintenance of Lists

The only way to know how well a system is working is to test it. One way to test the adequacy of VRD adding and maintenance processes is to corrupt a copy of the most recent VRD by seeding it with artificial records with names and other identifying information from lists of felons, deaths, and mentally incompetent people and with duplicate records of individuals already in the database but with realistic types of error in them. Once corrupted in this way, the VRD can be matched against all of the usual databases (DMV, felons, and so on) to see what fractions of the corruption in each category were detected, thus providing estimates of rates of false positives and false negatives. Because "ground truth" is known in the form of the original seedings, the fractions of detected corruption are likely to be reasonable estimates of the effectiveness of the process overall.[19]

A corollary of such testing is that those who receive the data resulting from such testing (ultimately, the public at large) must be educated to interpret the data in context—and specifically to understand that no procedure for adding or removing voters can be perfect. At the same time, there is nothing to suggest that individual voters who are wrongly eliminated from the VRD cannot complain or seek correction of the problem through existing channels that are available for resolving such problems.

Another possible approach to testing is to audit actual acceptance, rejection, and removal decisions, not just to verify that procedures have been followed but also to estimate error rates.

Take Steps to Minimize Errors During Data Entry

A number of steps can be taken to minimize data entry errors.

- Sample audits can be undertaken to assess the degree of the problem and to identify the source—some data entry personnel, for example, may be much less accurate than others. Some systems produce daily data entry reports that can be compared against the original card for errors; such systems are used in a number of jurisdictions.
- The registrant can be provided with a copy of the data that were actually entered (for example, when a voter receives his or her registration card, which should in most cases reflect all of the data entered on behalf of the voter), reminded to check the data, and given information on how to contact the election jurisdiction if there are errors on the card.
- During the input process, the entered values can be tested against domains (for example, common names, valid addresses including street name and postal code, valid phone numbers, valid dates of birth).
- Data can be entered twice by different people and compared for discrepancies (an expensive way to check, but effective in most instances).
- Discrepancies can be found when matching new inputs to previously known values (an ideal way to detect transposition keying errors in dates of birth, for example).

When errors or inconsistencies in the entered data are found, they should be immediately corrected. In some cases, an examination of the records themselves will indicate how corrections should be made; in other cases, it may be necessary to consult additional data sources or even the voter to make the necessary corrections. For example, the voter registrar might provide a special telephone number for voters to call to make corrections.

---

[19]However, note that even the best state-of-the-art "error generators" are not capable of generating the full range of errors encountered in real databases. Thus, these estimates are likely not to account for certain kinds of errors; as a result, actual performance in realistic settings could be expected to be different and probably somewhat worse.

The first two of these steps can be taken in the short term. The other three require a nontrivial amount of new technology deployment, and it is unlikely that they could be undertaken successfully in time for the November 2008 election.

Allow Selected Individuals to Suppress Address Information on Public Disclosures of Voter Registration Status

Although voter registration information is nominally public in most states, certain individuals (domestic violence victims, undercover police officers, witness protection program participants) have legitimate reasons for wanting to make address information inaccessible to the public, and an administrative process should be available to protect such information on request. Some privacy advocates might argue for the broadest possible scope of individuals who should be granted such privileges, but the committee is silent on this particular point.

Enacting this recommendation may require legislation in many jurisdictions; if so, it is probably not practical for 2008.

Encourage (but Do Not Require) Entities Sponsoring Voter Registration Drives to Submit Voter Registration Forms in a Timely Manner to Reduce Massive Influxes at the Registration Deadline

Voter registrar offices can be overwhelmed by the mechanics of data entry if large numbers of voter registration applications must be processed in a very short time. Such a volume reduces the time for error checking or multiple attempts to verify voter information, and often forces registrars to hire inexperienced temporary workers for data entry. These conditions in turn are likely to increase the error rate of data entry and may invalidate more registration applications than would be the case if more time were available to handle the applications.

POSSIBLE FUTURE IMPROVEMENTS THAT WILL REQUIRE LONGER-TERM ACTION

As indicated in the previous section, a number of improvements are possible in state VRDs that can only be implemented in a longer time frame than that provided by the November 2008 election. Some discussion of these improvements is included in this interim report to provide advice to states as they begin developing their priorities for voter registration databases for the 2010 elections and in next year's budgeting and planning process. In some cases, the improvements discussed will require a time-delimited investment associated with acquisition and deployment and a smaller stream of funding afterward; in other cases, they will require additional funding on a continuing basis as operating expenses. The committee's final report will address these longer-term recommendations in greater detail when needed.

Develop and Promote Public Access Portals for Online Checking of Voter Registration Status

In anticipation of being able to vote on Election Day, prospective voters may wish to check their voter registration status so that any irregularities can be corrected in time. Web-based portals for checking the state VRD increase the ability of individuals to do so. For example, such a portal may ask the user to provide a name, birth date, and Zip code, and return either the user's current registration status or an indication that there is no record on file that matches the information provided. Some jurisdictions already provide this service to voters today.

Such portals help to increase transparency in the VRD and will create another opportunity for the verification of voter information. They benefit individual voters who want to verify their information, and may provide an opportunity (if it is legal to do so, and if potential privacy concerns over retention of the data can be addressed) for third-party voter registration groups that wish to confirm that the applications they have collected have been received, processed, and accurately entered in the voter registration database.

States that have developed such portals (for example, Nevada[20] and Nebraska[21]) have generally integrated them into their voter registration Web sites. These portals must access information stored in a state's VRD, which means that their development requires some sensitivity to and technical capacity for dealing with security issues. For example, data compromises have been reported in other instances when live queries have been allowed access to the primary database, suggesting that it may be safer to implement some sort of buffered arrangement whereby the portal provides access only to a synchronized copy containing only the minimum amount of information.

Another point to be considered is the prevention of automated exploitation that might circumvent existing legal restrictions on making the voter registration database available to commercial users; automated tests that distinguish between human and automated responses (such as "captchas," which require the user to type the letters displayed in a distorted image) may be relevant in this regard, although this is an ongoing battle. Special steps must also be taken to prevent the display of voter registration information for individuals who need protection, such as victims of domestic abuse or individuals in witness protection, and in any event, the information to be displayed at all should be the minimum information needed for the voter to know that he or she is registered to vote and to inform the voter of the proper polling place (for example, driver's license numbers or SSNs (even SSN4) do not need to be displayed). Some states collect more information (for example, phone numbers, occupation, or e-mail addresses) on their application forms than is necessary for voter registration per se; such information poses increased privacy risks to the individual if needlessly disclosed.

Finally, for all states that provide online verification of voter registration information, it is important to inform voters that they should check their voter registration status well in advance of Election Day.

Some security issues are discussed in Appendix D.

Encourage/Require Departments of Motor Vehicles as Well as Public Assistance and Disability Service Agencies to Provide Voter Registration Information Electronically

The NVRA requires state DMVs, public assistance agencies, and disability service agencies to facilitate the voter registration process. Today, this facilitation is mostly paper-based. Automatically providing information on new applications or changes of address to voter registrars would significantly reduce the burden of maintaining VRDs by reducing requirements for manual data entry and updating registrations with new addresses.[22]

---

[20] See https://nvsos.gov/VoterSearch/.
[21] See https://www.votercheck.necvr.ne.gov/.
[22] This recommendation is consistent with the EAC's *Voluntary Guidance on Implementation of Statewide Voter Registration Lists*, III-D.2-d. This particular guidance notes that states should "ensure that the coordination of information in the verification process is accurate and efficient. Verification of voter registration information shall be accomplished through electronic transmission. Further, to the greatest extent allowed by State law and available technologies, this electronic transfer between statewide voter registration lists and coordinating, verification databases should be accomplished through direct, secure, interactive and integrated connections." See http://www.eac.gov/election/docs/statewide_registration_guidelines_072605.pdf/attachment_download/file.

As part of promoting cooperation and coordination between voter registrars and these other public service agencies, states may wish to develop and maintain performance metrics on the percentage of voter registration additions, modifications, and deletions that arrive electronically and on the number of electronic files that arrive from NVRA agencies that contain errors requiring correction. Such figures would provide a way of holding these agencies more accountable for their NVRA responsibilities.

The committee recognizes that election officials have no control over the budgets or operations of these agencies, a fact that often leads to a certain amount of bureaucratic politics as Agency A seeks to persuade Agency B to help carry out the mission of Agency A.

Encourage/Require Departments of Motor Vehicles, Public Assistance and Disability Service Agencies, Tax Assessors, and Other Public Service Agencies of State and Local Government in Their Communications with the Public to Remind Voters to Check and Update Their Information

Agencies of state and local government communicate with the public regularly, and each such communication is an opportunity to remind voters to check and update their information. Such reminders would entail little additional cost and could be helpful in increasing the accuracy and completeness of the data contained in VRDs.

Further, the online environment provides opportunities for less passive forms of reminder—for example, individuals who use online government services to indicate a change of address (for example, on tax or property assessment records) can be offered reminders to update their registration information, or can even be routed automatically to online voter registration services to effect a similar change of address. Note that such additions to the online environment for these other service agencies would be significantly less expensive than implementing the previous recommendation on developing and promoting portals for online checking of registration status and thus might well be a first long-term step that states could take.

Improve Matching Procedures

As noted in Appendix B, many (if not most) of the matching procedures used by the states have been developed on the basis of intuitive reasoning without further systematic validation or mathematically rigorous analysis, do not reflect the state of the art in matching techniques, and have not been validated in the market, scientifically, or otherwise. State-of-the-art matching techniques have been successfully used in a variety of commercial and government applications. The committee believes that there are several areas in which matching involving VRDs can be improved, and thus recommends that voter registrars engage the relevant technical community when considering improvements in matching techniques as described in the section "Improving Record-Level Matching" in Appendix B.

The enhanced methods should improve the capability for locating of duplicates in the VRD, the matching of voters against the state DMV file and the SSA files, and the matching of registered voters against any secondary federal or state list (for example, of deaths, felons, and so on). A demonstration of the effectiveness of these enhanced methods could be performed by applying them to a particular state's VRD file and showing how rates of false positives can be quite low even while significantly lowering rates of false negatives.

Establish a Software Repository of Tested Matching Algorithms

To support the adoption of improved matching procedures, a software repository of tested and debugged matching algorithms to which states had free access could reduce the burden on individual states to implement such procedures. A number of entities could provide such a repository, such as the EAC or the National Association of State Elections Directors.

Provide Voter Registration Receipts to Improve Administrative Processes

Voter registration cards should have a tear-off receipt, and online registrants should be told to make a copy of the online form as their receipts. Then the data should be kept by the states, and reported to the EAC, on how many individuals attempted to vote and were not registered but had their receipts. States should then be encouraged to lower that number.

In addition, the receipt might also include a tracking number or bar code to match it with the registration card itself, facilitating the association of specific individuals with specific forms. On the other hand, because including such a number or code would almost certainly have to be a government function, such numbers or codes might run afoul of the NVRA, which specifically allows private duplication of voter registration forms in order to facilitate their widest possible distribution. In addition, numbered forms entail additional costs for printing. Some states provide numbered registration forms today. The committee, however, takes no position on the general desirability of tracking numbers or codes at this time.

Although the use of these receipts is not intended to substitute for a proper voter registration or for provisional voting, such receipts would provide a factual basis for investigating, at least partially, claims from one political party that supporters of the other party had "pocketed" voter registration forms—that is, when conducting voter registration drives, receiving registrations for people of the opposite party and never turning them in. This activity is against the law, but there can be no proof as to whether it has occurred unless there is some form of receipt given to the person registering. If there were receipts, then people who possessed the receipts but were not in the VRD would be proof of some problem, including the possibility that registration forms had gone missing.

The committee recognizes that the NVRA (Section 8(a)(2)) already requires that election officials provide notice to applicants on the disposition of all voter registration applications. But this requirement can only be met when the applications indeed make it into the hands of these officials—if they never arrive, notice cannot be given, and individuals who never receive a notice cannot prove that they should have received notice.

Allow Voters to Register and to Update Missing or Incorrect Registration Information Online If a Signature Is Already on File with a State Agency

As noted in Appendix C, typographical errors could be reduced significantly by eliminating the data transcription process and importing most or all of the relevant data from another system and/or allowing the voter to enter data himself or herself when necessary. However, the voter will always have to provide at registration some means of authenticating himself or herself at the polls, such as a signature. A mail-in registration form can contain a box for the voter's signature, but online registration requires the applicant to appear (or to have appeared) somewhere in person at some official government agency to provide a signature. If this signature is digitized, it can be made available to the voter registrar along with the information needed to register to vote. A number of states today take advantage of the fact that their driver's licenses have signatures and have developed online registration portals that enable citizens with such licenses to register to vote online without having to appear in person anywhere.

Registration portals can also leverage the fact that basic information about the individual, such as name, address, birth date, and so on, is often also stored along with the signature—suggesting that importing the relevant data from the original state agency with the signature into the voter registration database is feasible in principle. When the voter registration application required information not already on file, the user would enter the information himself or herself and then be given a chance to verify and correct the information.

In addition, individuals whose registration forms contain illegible or missing information could be notified of that fact and at the same time be given a special code or password that would grant entry to a secure Web page, whereupon the individual could correct or provide the missing data. In the longer term, it might be possible to imagine real-time verification of a voter application, so that an applicant whose information did not match DMV or SSA information on file could be informed of that fact immediately, so that corrections could be made at the moment.

Develop Procedures for Handling Disenfranchisement Caused by Mistaken Removals from Voter Registration Lists

Any given removal of a name from a voter registration list may have been performed in error. Indeed, a great deal of experience with information technology suggests that even a combination of automated and human matching can sometimes result in inappropriate action because of data errors, inherent ambiguity in the data, algorithm deficiencies, human error, and so on. For example, a felony may have been reduced to a misdemeanor by the court without that fact being made known to election officials. Other sources of error exist as well, and there is an inherent unfairness in changing a voter's status and potentially disenfranchising him or her without providing an opportunity for contesting the removal.

Procedures for addressing disenfranchisement could be handled in a number of different ways. For example, one approach is to provide the person removed from a voter registration list with the opportunity to contest that decision before the removal is made final. Yet small election offices might find this approach onerous in light of small staffs, high mailing costs, and other pertinent issues. In addition, notification of voters removed from the list may be upsetting to the families of those individuals suffering from the pain of a relative's death or being declared mentally incompetent. Another approach might be to allow a voter disenfranchised by being removed to vote provisionally. Such an approach is mandated by HAVA for federal elections, but it could be adopted for state and local elections as well.

Developing such procedures might well require new legislation and administrative processes.

Improve the Design of Voter Registration Forms

The design of forms has a significant impact on their usability and their ability to capture the data that the form filler intends to record. For example, providing a specific separate space for each letter/number of the name/address often improves the legibility of forms completed, and may improve the suitability of the filled-out form for processing by optical character recognition software. However, form design is often challenging and generally requires a significant degree of empirical testing to assess the usability of any given design.[23]

---

[23] An informative reference on the design of forms for use by election officials is Marcia Lausen, *Design for Democracy: Ballot and Election Design*, University of Chicago Press and American Institute of Graphic Arts, 2007.

Appendixes

A

Background and Context

THE ROLE AND STRUCTURE OF VOTER REGISTRATION

Voter registration (described briefly in Box A.1) plays a central role in elections in most states. Today, in all states except one (North Dakota), a voter must be registered for his or her vote to count in an election; some states allow same-day voter registration on Election Day.

During reforms of the Progressive era, voter registration procedures spread throughout the states, beginning in urban areas, launched at least in part in an attempt to reform how elections were carried out. These reforms aimed to restore fairness in the conduct of elections by, for example, minimizing the influence of urban political machines over elections. However, many believe that these procedures also caused voter turnout to decline sharply. The use of strict registration rules to verify the eligibility of a voter, such as requiring in-person registration during limited weekday hours, effectively limited the participation of many eligible voters who could not afford to take time off work to register to vote.[1] These rules were eventually eased by a series of federal mandates.

The U.S. Constitution (Article I, Section 4 and Article II, Section I) gives states the power to make rules governing federal elections, subject to the authority of Congress to make or alter such rules. Amendments to the Constitution prohibit racial discrimination in the right to vote or gender, prohibit poll taxes, and grant individuals the right to vote at age 18. The one-person, one-vote principle emerges mainly from Supreme Court interpretations of the equal protection clause of the 14th Amendment and subsequent legislation.

In addition, starting with the 1960s civil rights legislation, Congress gradually expanded federal oversight of election administration and registration provisions, although states continue to have considerable discretion in how to implement federal requirements. The Voting Rights Act of 1965 aims to broadly protect voter rights by prohibiting discriminatory voting practices and by preventing an individual from being denied the right to vote "because of an error or omission on any record or paper relating to any application, registration, or other act requisite to voting, if such error or omission is not material in determining whether such individual is qualified under the State law to vote in such election." Subsequent legislation aimed at facilitating voter registration and increasing the accessibility of absentee ballots for particular classes of voters includes the Voting Accessibility for the Elderly and Handicapped Act of 1984 and the Uniformed and Overseas Citizen Absentee Voting Act of 1986.

The National Voter Registration Act of 1994 (NVRA) added two requirements to voter registration. The first was to increase voter registrations by requiring applications to be made available at a number of physical locations—motor vehicle agencies, all offices that provide public assistance or services to persons with disabilities, other places that states could designate (for example, public libraries), and nongovernmental offices that agree to serve as voter registration sites—and by mail. The second focused on the maintenance of voter lists by establishing rules under which names could be removed from the voter registration list. It also mandated that states monitor and report on their

---

[1] A. Keyssar, *The Right to Vote: The Contested History of Democracy in the United States*, Basic Books, New York, 2000.

> **BOX A.1**
> **A Thumbnail Description of Voter Registration**
>
> States generally require that a voter be a U.S. citizen, at least 18 years of age, and a resident (in some cases, a resident for some minimum period of time, such as 30 days). Some states also limit voter eligibility on the basis of criminal status (for example, incarcerated felons may not be permitted to vote), and some on the basis of mental competency, although the specifics of these limitations vary.[1]
>
> As a general rule, a voter registers to vote in a specific geographic jurisdiction that is determined from the residential address that he or she provides for the purpose of voting. Citizens can register to vote at election offices. Depending on the state, citizens can also obtain voter registration materials in many places, including military facilities, assisted living facilities, high schools, vocational schools, social service agencies, nursing homes, and libraries, or through voter registration drives, or by downloading materials from the Internet. In addition, the National Voter Registration Act requires all states to provide such materials at their departments of motor vehicles, departments of human services, and public assistance agencies. By filling out the required forms and providing the necessary identification, citizens in all states can also register to vote by mail. In at least two states (Washington and Arizona), a citizen can register to vote through the Internet if he or she already has a driver's license or a state-issued ID from that state.
>
> The voter completes the registration form and it is returned to the election office. The returned materials are accompanied by an original signature that serves as an authentication mechanism when voter registration must be checked in the future. If the voter registers at a department of motor vehicles, the relevant information may be extracted from the information on file or provided at the department of motor vehicles (DMV) and transmitted electronically to the election office, along with the signature on file with the DMV as an authentication device for the voter at the polls. Overseas voters, and members of the U.S. armed forces and their dependents, can sometimes register to vote by fax.
>
> The voting address of record determines the precinct from which the voter may cast his or her ballot, whether at the polling place, or by absentee or mail ballot, or by an early vote. A precinct is a subdivision of a local election jurisdiction, and all voters in a given precinct vote at one polling place. (Sometimes, a number of small precincts are consolidated at one polling place, and sometimes election officials can require that all voters from certain precincts vote by mail.) A local election jurisdiction is an administrative entity responsible for the conduct and administration of elections within it, and may be a county or a municipality (a city or town).
>
> ---
> [1] A description of the legal restrictions on felons and voting rights in a large number of states can be found in American Civil Liberties Union, *Purged! How Flawed and Inconsistent Voting Systems Could Deprive Millions of Americans of the Right to Vote*, October 2004, available at http://www.aclu.org/VotingRights/VotingRights.cfm?ID=16845&c=167.
> SOURCE: Adapted largely from National Research Council, *Asking the Right Questions About Electronic Voting*, Richard Celeste, Dick Thornburgh, and Herbert Lin (eds.), The National Academies Press, Washington, D.C., 2005.

implementation of the NVRA. Figure A.1 illustrates the various list maintenance options under the NVRA.

Following the passage of the NVRA, a variety of proposals were made to further enhance voter registration by the creation of centralized statewide voter registration databases. Following the Florida recount in the 2000 presidential election, the Help America Vote Act (HAVA) was passed in 2002 to undertake a number of electoral reforms.

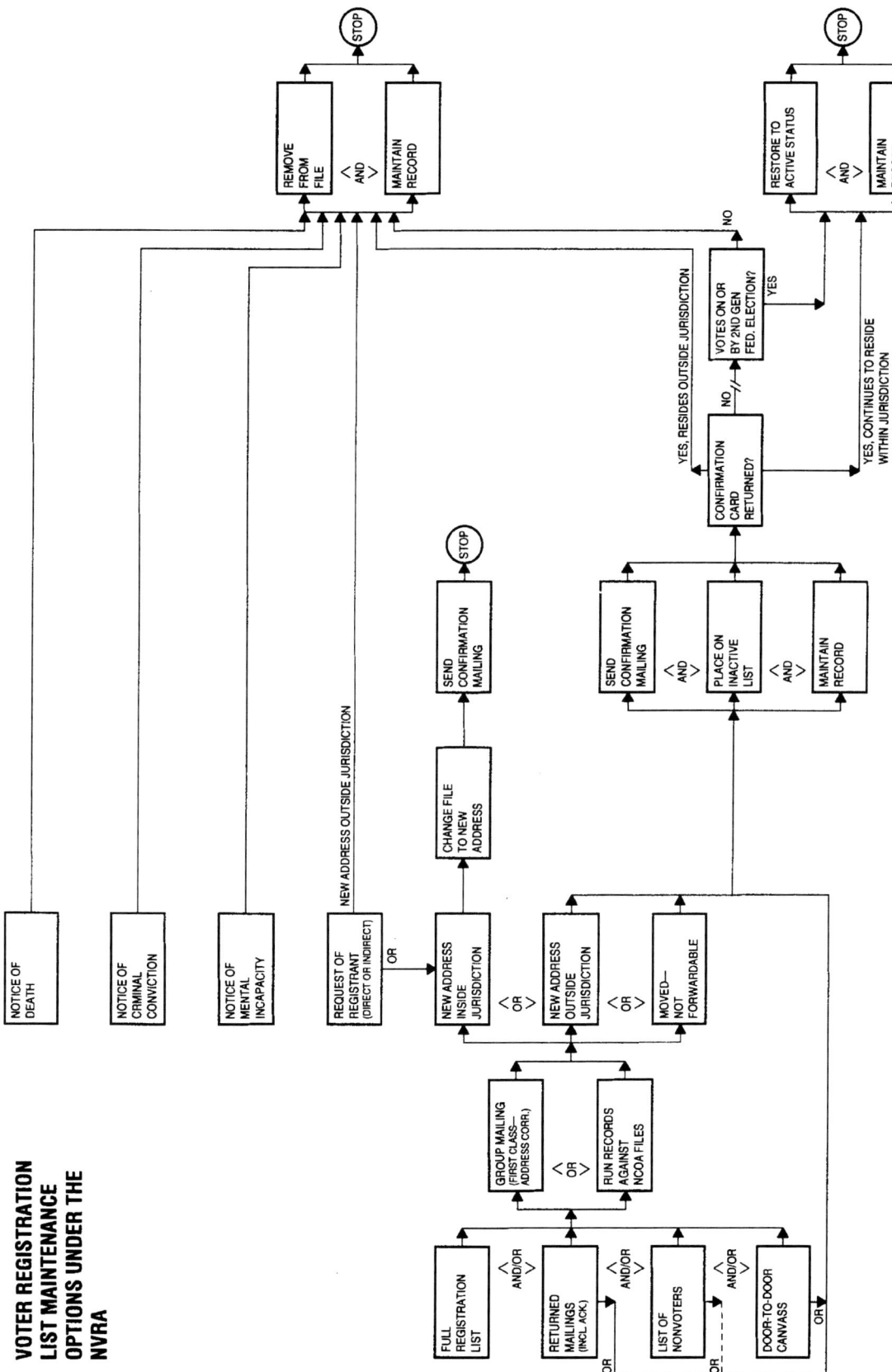

FIGURE A.1 Voter registration list maintenance options under the National Voter Registration Act. SOURCE: National Clearinghouse on Election Administration, "Implementing the National Voter Registration Act of 1993: Requirements, Issues, Approaches, and Examples," Federal Election Commission, Washington, D.C., January 1, 1994, p. 5-1.

HAVA aimed to improve election administration by allocating funds to upgrade and certify voting systems and by creating the U.S. Election Assistance Commission (EAC) to provide voluntary guidance to states. Another goal of HAVA was to establish more uniformity within individual states and to empower the states to take a stronger role vis-à-vis local election officials. Finally, HAVA included several provisions related to voter registration databases. It required states to shift to centralized voter registration lists at the state level and away from the estimated 3,000, mostly locally administered, voter registration lists. It requires that each state's database contain the name and registration information of each legally registered voter in the state and that each legally registered voter be assigned a unique identifier. HAVA specifies that the state list is the official voter registration list for federal elections. It also requires election officials to perform regular maintenance regarding the accuracy and completeness of the registration lists.[2]

THE POLITICAL LANDSCAPE OF VOTER REGISTRATION

The tensions that gave rise to laws related to voter registration persist today. In an ideal world, voter registration lists would include all those individuals eligible to vote and none of the individuals not eligible to vote. In addition, all of the data in the database would be factually correct. For purposes of this report, the term "accuracy" refers to the factual correctness of the data that exist in the database and also the notion that the database contains none of the individuals not eligible to vote. Completeness refers to the presence in the database of all individuals who *should* be in the database. If the database is perfect, it is both 100 percent accurate and 100 percent complete—that is, all of the data in the database are correct (and thus the database contains no individual who should not be in the database), *and* the database includes all of the individuals who should be in the database. Notice that in this formulation, accuracy does *not* subsume completeness, so that a database must be characterized with respect to *both* attributes.

It is often true in practice that efforts to maximize in the voter registration database (VRD) the number of individuals eligible to vote conflict with efforts to minimize the number of individuals in the VRD who are *not* eligible to vote. One view of this tension emphasizes the risks of voter fraud and highlights the need to maintain the integrity of the voting list by placing the greatest effort on minimizing the number of individuals in the VRD who are *not* eligible to vote. This side argues that if election fraud were to occur, it could undermine public confidence in an election.

A different view of these tensions emphasizes the importance of inclusivity in a representative democracy. Individuals with these concerns believe that the number of eligible but unregistered voters could be decreased through better access to and easier voter registration procedures. This side contends that confidence in the election process could be lost if methods and procedures used to improve the accuracy of voter registration lists cause eligible voters to be removed erroneously, and that overly strict or onerous procedures could suppress registering and/or voting. Additionally, there is concern that the barrier of registration might skew a representative government toward certain interests because the political views and values of those who do not vote as a result of registration issues may differ from those of individuals who do vote. Completeness serves the end of inclusivity by ensuring that all eligible individuals who have sought to register to vote are not erroneously deleted from the VRD.

These two views are commonly identified with specific political parties. Another set of concerns about voter registration, generally not associated with one party or another, stems from the fact that exercising the right to vote in the United States requires the active participation of the voter to register—and some individuals in policy-making or operational positions have been known to be dismissive of efforts to ease the voter registration process or to reduce voter effort in maintaining registration by saying, in effect, "If the person isn't willing to do X, then he or she shouldn't be voting anyway."

---

[2]HAVA uses the term "accuracy" to mean a list both from which ineligible individuals have been eliminated and for which safeguards have been established to ensure that eligible individuals have not been improperly eliminated.

Ultimately, voter registration lists cannot be perfect with respect to either completeness or accuracy, in part because the voting population changes by the day and even by the hour. But today's political environment raises the stakes significantly for even small deviations from perfection in either direction. Today's political campaigns and debates are rancorous and bitter. In addition, many elections today are close—a reflection of an electorate that has been about evenly divided—and close elections are breeding grounds for postelection suspicion, on the theory that even a small amount of fraud or accident or mishap or improperly followed procedure might have tipped the election the other way. While the presidential election of 2000 is perhaps the most salient example, outcomes in other close races have been very closely scrutinized by supporters of the losing side for irregularities in all aspects of the voting process, including voter registration.

These tensions and political sensitivities point to the need for voter registration procedures and practices that are transparent, consistent, and robust, and for the use of approaches that balance the inherent tensions. This report does not aim to resolve these tensions, but they must be kept in mind as technical, policy, and procedural challenges of implementing and maintaining statewide voter registration databases are considered.

OTHER USES OF VOTER REGISTRATION LISTS

Voter registration lists are used for a number of purposes other than establishing the eligibility of an individual to vote in an election. For example, voter registration lists are used by candidates and political parties to reach out to potential voters by phone and by mail. At the local level, they are used to estimate the financial, personnel, and logistical requirements for elections. They are used to track absentee ballots and voter histories. They are used in some jurisdictions to establish signature and vote thresholds for referenda and petitions. They are used, at least in part, to establish jury pools. All of these uses require voter registration information to be as accurate and complete as possible.

Some of these applications have led to privacy concerns, and although most voter registration data are generally public information, there are sometimes restrictions on making such information broadly available. For example, some states restrict the sale or use of voter registration lists for commercial solicitation purposes. Concerns have also been raised about the safety of battered men or women if the contact information contained in their voter registration were to be disclosed publicly, and some jurisdictions have enacted special protections in this instance.

THE BASIC REQUIREMENT FOR STATEWIDE VOTER REGISTRATION DATABASES

HAVA Section 303 requires each state to establish and maintain a "single, uniform, official, centralized, interactive computerized statewide voter registration list" that contains the voter registration information for all eligible voters in the state and requires that the VRD be electronically accessible by any election official in the state. But although HAVA provides some criteria for developing and maintaining this database, and the Election Assistance Commission has issued its 2005 *Voluntary Guidance on Implementation of Statewide Voter Registration Lists*,[3] the states still maintain a degree of discretion in how to conform to HAVA. Such discretion, exercised in different ways by different states, inevitably leads to various problems and inconsistencies within and between statewide voter registration databases.

States have taken different architectural approaches to building systems to meet the centralized voter registration list requirement. Under the so-called top-down approach followed by many states, state election officials maintain a single, unified database and local election officials provide the state with the

---

[3] Available at http://www.eac.gov/election/docs/statewide_registration_guidelines_072605.pdf/attachment_download/file.

information needed to update the database. Some states instead opted for a bottom-up approach, in which local jurisdictions continue to maintain their own registration lists but also provide periodic updates to a separate statewide system. Other states have adopted a hybrid architecture that combines elements of both the top-down and the bottom-up approach. Kentucky and Michigan had already implemented statewide voter registration databases before the enactment of HAVA, but most states have had to implement new systems to comply with HAVA.

Does HAVA mandate a particular architectural approach to the implementation of VRDs? This issue has been argued both in the affirmative and in the negative at length, and the committee takes no position on this question. HAVA does require that the control of the VRD be maintained at the statewide level. Thus, the committee believes that the particular technical architecture used is less significant than the structure of the actual workflow used within a state. For instance, a county or municipality that remains in full control over the registration process and over who is on or off the voting rolls is not comporting itself within the spirit of HAVA, which mandates statewide control. As a result, any assessment of whether a system conforms to the requirements and expectations of HAVA should consider the processes whereby information is entered into the system, verified, and maintained.

It should also be noted that although guidance regarding database structures or system attributes has been promulgated through the EAC's *Voluntary Guidance on Implementation of Statewide Voter Registration Lists*,[4] the guidance remains voluntary, and the agency charged with enforcing HAVA—the Department of Justice—has not issued guidelines or regulations of its own. Thus, state election officials may proceed at their own risk that some design decision might be challenged later as not being HAVA-compliant.

---

[4] Available at http://www.eac.gov/election/docs/statewide_registration_guidelines_072605.pdf/attachment_download/file.

B

Matching Records Across Databases

As noted in Appendix A, HAVA and the NVRA direct the states to implement a variety of procedures that require the "coordination" of voter registration databases (VRDs) with other databases. The central technical issue in such coordination (known in this appendix as "matching" or, more precisely, record-level matching) is finding individuals who are represented in both the VRD and another database (or the reverse—finding an individual who is represented in only one of these databases). (In the case of removing duplicate registrations, the "coordination" occurs within the same database.)

THE BASIC PROCESS OF MATCHING RECORDS ACROSS DATABASES WITHOUT UNIQUE IDENTIFIERS[1]

The basic element of a VRD is a record with data contained within specific fields associated with an individual—first name, last name, street address, date of birth, and so on. Databases may differ in the number of fields that a given record contains (for example, one database may include a field for telephone number and another might not) or in definitions of the fields (for example, one database may have one field for street name and number together (123 Main Street), and another may have separate fields for street name (Main Street) and street number (123).

Matching records across databases (that is, record-level matching) involves the comparison of corresponding fields between databases. HAVA requires states to verify the information provided on a new voter registration application by verifying the applicable information with the state's motor vehicle agency, in the case of a driver's license, or with the Social Security Administration (SSA), to verify the last four digits of the Social Security number. Individual states also have the authority to—and often do—use additional databases and criteria to verify voter registration information.[2]

The matching process is greatly simplified if each individual has used the same unique identifier (such as the driver's license number or the full Social Security number) in each database.[3] In this case, matching records across databases is simplified. However, in the absence of a unique identifier, it is necessary to use combinations of fields in order to match records. Matches based on the comparison of corresponding fields such as first name, last name, address, and date of birth are inherently inferential, and thus subject to higher rates of error. (Some combinations, such as first name, last name, date of birth,

---

[1] For an overall background document that covers many elementary aspects of matching records (that is, record linkage), see William E. Winkler, "Matching and Record Linkage," pp. 355-384 in *Business Survey Methods*, Brenda G. Cox et al. (eds.), Wiley, New York, 1995.

[2] See Election Assistance Commission, *Impact of the National Voter Registration Act on Federal Elections 2005-2006*, Table 12, "Verification of Applications," p. 72, available at http://www.eac.gov/clearinghouse/docs/the-impact-of-the-national-voter-registration-act-on-federal-elections-2005-2006/attachment_download/file.

[3] In fact, even the full SSN is flawed as a unique identifier, as the SSA has been known from time to time to issue the same SSN to different individuals. Identity theft in which an individual appropriates someone else's SSN has also happened. Lastly, because the SSN lacks a check digit and is most often entered manually (rather than swiped as credit cards are), typographical errors often occur with no way of catching identifying them at the point of entry.

and last four digits of the Social Security number, have a high likelihood of uniquely identifying an individual.[4])

Errors in record-level matching may be false positives (a match is indicated when in fact the two records refer to different individuals) or false negatives (a nonmatch is indicated when the two records refer to the same individual). What is an acceptable upper limit on a given type of error depends on the application in question. For example, if the voter registration database is being checked against a database of felons or dead people, a low rate of false positives is needed to reduce the likelihood that eligible voters are removed from the VRD. Just how low a rate is acceptable is a policy choice.

In this report, the term "field-level match" denotes the process of comparing individual fields, so that the "first name" field of a record in Database 1 is compared to the "first name" field of a record in Database 2. In addition, a field-level match can be indicated on the basis of different match rules, which might include:

- Exact match—the fields are exactly equal, character by character for every character.
- Fuzzy or approximate match, which is intended to deal with typographical variation. At its simplest level, it allows comparison of fields with very simple errors ("Smith" versus "Smoth"). Fuzzy matching methods can be developed intuitively as seems to be the case in many VRD applications or based on principles that computer scientists have shown to work consistently well in practice.
- Content equivalence—"Road" and "Rd," or "Bill" and "William" are treated as equal.

The need for such rules arises for many reasons, not the least of which is that when asked for information, people often provide inconsistent information unintentionally. They use nicknames, include or omit middle initials, use abbreviations or not, and so on—and forget what they have done on previous occasions. An area code for a phone number may have changed. A street address might be recorded with digits transposed in the house number, or a street name spelled incorrectly, or with the wrong Zip code.

A record-level match occurs when several field-level matches are indicated. The decision about how many field-level matches are needed to define a record-level match is an important influence on the accuracy of the match. For example, a record-level match rule that required only field-level matches on first name and last name would lead to many more false positives than a rule requiring field-level matches on first name, last name, and date of birth. If the former rule were used instead of the latter to remove voters from registration lists (for example, if the voter registration list were compared against a list of state felons), many more eligible voters would be improperly removed.[5] (In principle and sometimes in practice, matching algorithms can also consider differences as well as similarities. For example, if the

---

[4] One way to estimate how many combinations exist is to consider that the population of the United States is currently approximately 300 million. The number of possible four-digit SSNs is 10,000. A plausible estimate of the number of distinct birth dates (month, day, year) is perhaps $365 \times 70 = \sim 25,000$. Thus, there are around 250 million possible combinations of birth date and four-digit SSN, which corresponds approximately to about one such combination for every American.

[5] An example of such a problem was a case with a record-level match conducted to identify felons in the voter registration database in Florida before the 2000 election. In matching the Florida VRD to a national list of felons, the applicable rule used exact field-level matches on the first four letters of the first name, middle initial, gender, and last four digits of the Social Security number (when available) and used approximate matches for last name (matching on 80 percent of the letters in the last name) and date of birth. Certain name variations were also explicitly taken into account (Willie could match William; John Richard could match Richard John). The result of this match was that approximately 15 percent of the names removed from the VRD were improperly removed. See Gregory Palast, "The Wrong Way to Fix the Vote," *The Washington Post*, Sunday, June 10, 2001, Outlook section, p. 1, available at http://www.legitgov.org/palast_wrong_way_fix_vote.html. To remediate the issues raised in this case, Choicepoint—the firm responsible for conducting the match—agreed to a very detailed set of criteria described in Box B.1.

BOX B.1
The Detailed Nature of Match Criteria—An Illustration

As an illustration of the detail with which match criteria must be specified, consider the following criteria taken from the consent decree in *National Association for the Advancement of Colored People v. Katherine Harris, Secretary of State of Florida et al.* (Case No. 01-120-CIV-Gold/Simonton, United States District Court, for the Southern District of Florida).

Notice of Filing Fully Executed Copy of June 28, 2002, Choicepoint Settlement Agreement . . .

9. The matching criteria described in Paragraph A.8 . . . [are] as follows:

ChoicePoint will identify all matches on the comprehensive list resulting from the processing described in Paragraphs A.2-A.7 that do not match based on all of the following data fields:

- Validated 9 digit Social Security Number
- Non-normalized (i.e., as name appears in original source data) Last Name
- Non-normalized (i.e., as name appears in original source data) First Name
- Non-normalized (i.e., as name appears in original source data) Middle Name
- Suffix
- Race
- Gender
- Date of Birth

ChoicePoint will perform Social Security Number validation in accordance with guidelines established by the Social Security Administration.

Records will be deemed to match under the criteria listed above if a middle name in one record begins with the same letter as a middle initial shown in the match record assuming all other fields listed above match.

Records will be deemed not to match under the criteria listed above if they share common blank data fields among the fields listed above, except for cases in which the middle name field or suffix field is blank in both records.

Records will be deemed not to match under the criteria listed above if one of the fields being compared contains data and the same field in the match record contains no data.

---

name and date of birth are the same but the Social Security number and gender values are inconsistent between the records, a nonmatch might be indicated under some circumstances.)

States have considerable discretion to decide for themselves the criteria to be used for matching, although these criteria cannot be used to disenfranchise legitimate voters.[6] Some states will use fuzzy matching and others exact matching for checking any given data field. States also vary in the fields that they check—for example, some will compare addresses and others will not. In general, some election offices may be using match criteria without sufficient consideration of possible false-positive and false-negative error rates with any variants of the methods.

---

[6] A description of the various practices employed by the various states in late 2005 can be found in Wendy Weiser, Justin Levitt, and Ana Munoz, *Making the List: Database Matching and Verification Processes for Voter Registration*, Brennan Center, New York University, 2006, available at http://www.brennancenter.org/dynamic/subpages/download_file_49479.pdf.

Finally, a manual review of matches is sometimes performed. That is, under some circumstances, a voter registrar will review a match (or a nonmatch) indicated by automated processes.

COMPLICATIONS IN MATCHING

Apart from the issues involved in the matching criteria, a variety of data issues also complicate matching. Data quality (addressed in more detail in Appendix C) is impaired by many different sources of error, including illegible handwriting, incomplete or lost forms, and keypunching errors.

Another problem occurs because certain names are quite common. For example, it is known that the name "John Smith" occurs between 30,000 and 60,000 times in national lists. This means that there are between 1.5 and 3.0 John Smith's for each date of birth. Assuming there are 500 individuals named John Smith in a given state, then a certain (low) proportion of them will have the same date of birth. With certain other commonly occurring names, some chance agreements on dates of birth would be expected as well.[7]

This point suggests that more accurate record-level matching will take into account the possibility of chance agreement on date of birth for certain commonly occurring combinations of first and last name, which will in turn require knowledge of the most common names in any given state. Such information can easily be computed from either state-held databases (such as the department of motor vehicles (DMV) or voter registration databases, whichever is of higher quality as indicated by fewer typographical errors, more current entries, and so on) or commercially available databases (such as credit header records[8]).

Matches involving common names may require additional processing (perhaps manual) and involve the use of additional information not contained in databases. For instance, a prior address may confirm a match on a name when date of birth is missing. An e-mail address, phone number, or other corroborating information may confirm a match when there is typographical error in any of the first name, last name, or date of birth.

At the same time, using other fields may entail other complications. For example, addresses may be represented differently in different databases; for example, in one database, "123 Main Street" represents an address, whereas in another database, addresses are represented in three fields (house number ("123"), street name ("Main"), and suffix ("Street")). Address standardization is often required to fix this problem.

Finally, the above technically oriented comments *presume* that the databases to be matched against the VRD are in fact available. But in the real world of state voter registration databases, fragmented state control over state social service agencies and departments of motor vehicles, and state/county tensions regarding authority over voter registration, the politics of database availability are at least as challenging as the technology for matching. Achieving integration or interoperability of the information systems of election officials and of other state and/or local agencies may be deeply problematic if strong political leadership is not available to demand cooperation. Database-providing agencies not under the authority of state election officials (whether state or county) may well give low priority to meeting the election needs of the state, resulting in difficulties for state election officials in gaining access without undue delay or difficulty. For example, a database-providing agency may demand that election officials provide a voter registration list in a particular format that is hard or time-consuming to generate before the agency is willing to perform a match between the two databases. A more serious problem occurs when the database-providing agency is made responsible for matching the voter registration data against its own data—the agency may be unable to devote serious resources to doing so,

---

[7] See, for example, Michael P. McDonald, "The True Electorate: A Cross-Validation of Voter File and Election Poll Demographics," *Public Opinion Quarterly* 71(4):588-602, 2007.

[8] Credit headers refer to information in the credit report such as name, address, and phone number, not the credit history portion of the report.

APPENDIX B

or lack the inclination or skills to do the matching properly. An agency may be unmotivated to resolve or address possible interoperability problems.

THE POSSIBLE IMPACT OF INADEQUATE RECORD-LEVEL MATCHING

According to the EAC report *Impact of the National Voter Registration Act on Federal Elections 2005-2006*,[9] there were 36,277,749 voter applications received by 45 reporting states. Among those received, there were 10,938,385 changes of address or party; 2,196,608 duplicate applications; and 1,138,955 invalid or rejected applications—resulting in a total of 17,281,234 new registrants.[10] The percentage of applications not entered into the database because they were "invalid or rejected" or "duplicate applications" was about 9 percent, a total of 3,335,563 in the 45 reporting states. For comparison purposes, Table 4b from page 50 of the EAC report indicates that 333,663 people from 34 reporting states were removed from voter registration lists due to presumed felony convictions.

Once it is known that an application is not a duplicate, and not just a change of address or party, the application needs to be verified. Table 12, "Verification of Applications," on page 72 in the EAC report[11] shows that each state has its own unique set of criteria for verifying the applications, ranging from states like Pennsylvania, which verifies only through the DMV and the SSA, to Montana, which verifies against the DMV, the SSA, Vital Records, "Match Against Voter Registration Databases," "Tracking Returned Voter ID Cards," "Tracking Returned Disposition Notices," and "Verify Through Other Agency." According to Table 13, "Data Fields for Comparison to Identify Duplications," in the EAC report, 15 states verify using the address; 48 verify the date of birth; 38 verify the driver's license number; 46 verify the names provided by the registrant; 40 verify "Social Security number" (although surely that is just the last four digits in most cases, since according to Table 11, pages 68-69, in the EAC report, only 7 states use the full SSN); and 10 verify "other" data.

Consider two points. First, the state with the highest rate of "invalid or rejected" applications (Table 3, p. 38, in the EAC report) also reported in this survey that it verifies application information only through the DMV and the SSA (Table 12). Second, the state reporting in this survey the highest percentage of applications rejected because they were duplicates also reports in this survey that it uses only date of birth and names provided by the applicant to identify duplications (Table 13 in the EAC report). These points do not prove a causal relationship between use of a small number of non-VRD databases or a small number of fields in verification and a high percentage of rejected applications, but presuming that the data reported are valid and accurately reported, these points raise the question of how a broader set of criteria would have changed the percentage of applications rejected.[12]

---

[9] Available at http://www.eac.gov/clearinghouse/docs/the-impact-of-the-national-voter-registration-act-on-federal-elections-2005-2006/attachment_download/file.

[10] The EAC report also notes that it "may also have under-reported various voter registration activities because several States were in the middle of converting their local voter registration files into a statewide system in 2005. As a result, some States indicated that their local jurisdictions stopped keeping track of various registration functions and activities because they understood the State would be compiling this information" (p. 10).

[11] In this and the next paragraph, the tables (and page numbers) referred to are in the EAC report *Impact of the National Voter Registration Act on Federal Elections 2005-2006*, available at http://www.eac.gov/clearinghouse/docs/the-impact-of-the-national-voter-registration-act-on-federal-elections-2005-2006/attachment_download/file.

[12] The committee recognizes that the issue of data validity is an important one. For example, states may have reported their figures using definitions or criteria that were not uniform across all reporting jurisdictions. Issues with terminology are also known to cause difficulties for survey design. Until such matters are resolved, these data can only be regarded as providing tentative indications of possible relationships.

AN IMPORTANT EXAMPLE OF MATCHING IN PRACTICE

To illustrate the issues described above, consider a record-level match based on exact matches for an individual's first and last name, the month and year of birth, and the last four digits of an SSN. This example is significant because HAVA requires the Social Security Administration to verify the name, date of birth and the last four digits of the SSN ("the applicable information") in support of the federal voting process (usually to verify information for first-time voter applicants who do not provide a driver's license number to be checked against state DMV records), and to notify the voter registrar if the person so identified is deceased. (This requirement does not mean that the SSA mechanism is the only means through which voter information can be verified—states with other mechanisms available to them can select another method. According to the Brennan Center, 24 states in late 2005 planned to use the process described above.[13])

The requirement of using only the last four digits of the SSN increases the number of false positives, even though the absolute number of false positives is still quite low. The limitation to the use of the last four digits of the SSN reflects a balancing between a more effective matching of records and concerns about privacy.

Upon receipt of the applicable information, the SSA queries its database and returns one of five responses: no match found; one unique match, death indicator absent; one unique match, death indicator present; multiple matches found with at least one lacking a death indicator; multiple matches found but all with death indicator. As noted above, the query is based on searching for exact matches on the applicable information. At its November 2007 workshop, the committee heard testimony that this particular strategy for matching was developed by the SSA through the efforts of a working group involving the National Association of Secretaries of State, National Association of State Election Directors, American Association of Motor Vehicle Administrators, and five states. However, to the best of the committee's knowledge, no testing of match criteria was conducted in advance of deployment, and the error rates that such a strategy would entail were unknown at the time of deployment.

This strategy has a number of limitations that would prevent records from being matched when they should be matched. For example, the search query does not account for content equivalence of names (so that Bill and William are regarded as completely different names). Using only the first and last name causes difficulty, because the number of multiple and compound names is increasing rapidly in the population. In addition, a full legal name was not originally required to obtain an SSN, and thus many SSA records do not contain the full legal names of individuals. Changes in last name (for example, of women who change their last names through marriage) are also problematic, as someone may not report a change of last name to the SSA until it is needed to determine Social Security benefits. In addition, individuals were not required until 1972 to provide SSA proof of identity when applying for an SSN. Finally, individuals may still have been assigned SSNs even if their applications did not contain birth date information.

Data provided by the SSA to the committee's second workshop in November 2007 indicate that 55 percent of queries result in at least one match being indicated; queries using the full SSN result in a match rate of about 88 percent. The cost per query is at less than one cent ($.0062), which is low enough to allow election officials to vary the queries themselves in the event that a nonmatch response is received (for example, querying on "Bill" if "William" did not return a match).

---

[13]Wendy Weiser, Justin Levitt, and Ana Munoz, *Making the List: Database Matching and Verification Processes for Voter Registration*, Brennan Center, New York University, 2006, available at http://www.brennancenter.org/dynamic/subpages/download_file_49479.pdf.

As an example of a matching procedure in action, consider the elements of a new voter registration application card as shown on the left below and the SSA record on the right (presume these records are, in fact, supposed to refer to the same person):

> *New Registration Card* *SSA Record*
>
> Tom T Bowden Taylor T Bowden
> 3121 Escondido Way
> 11/04/77 11/04/77
> SSN 000001087 SSN 000001087

In this case, the SSA would return a response of "no match found." However, if the voter registrar could determine that either Tom has a middle name of Taylor or Taylor has a middle name of Tom or Thomas, then this registrar could associate these records with some degree of confidence if he or she concluded that the first and middle names have been transposed. But in the absence of other information, the registrar has no way to make such a determination.

States vary in their treatment of what happens in the event that an applicant's information cannot be matched against the SSA or DMV databases. In some cases, a state may grant the applicant a conditional registration that requires the voter to present an ID at the polls before voting (indeed, in some states, all first-time voters are required to present an ID at the polls, regardless of whether a match is found); others may provide a provisional ballot to the voter on election day. At the time of this writing, a Washington state law that requires a nonmatch to result in an applicant not being registered is being challenged.[14]

IMPROVING RECORD-LEVEL MATCHING

In general, three approaches can be used to improve record-level matching: allowing more data (that is, using more data fields or more complete data fields in performing the match), improving the quality of the data contained in the relevant databases (including the use of tertiary/external data), and introducing systematic field-level matching algorithms to augment certain locally developed matching techniques.

The first approach often runs afoul of privacy concerns, and it requires policy makers to be willing to make a tradeoff between less privacy and better record-level matching. In this case, experiments with using more data fields or more complete data fields are necessary to determine the incremental benefit in record-level matching (for example, adding another field or using the last six digits of the SSN instead of only the last four). The second approach, improving data quality, is addressed in more detail in Appendix C.

For purposes of this report, "ad hoc matching" is used to mean matching developed on the basis of intuitive reasoning that is not further validated systematically or analyzed with mathematical rigor. By contrast, systematic matching is based on a formal mathematical approach that develops metrics to measure match efficacy. With metrics in hand, policy makers can set scales for three relevant areas—what determines a match, what determines a nonmatch, and what is indeterminate. Implementation of systematic techniques for matching can use some or all of the following elements:

---

[14]See *Washington Association of Churches v. Reed*, No. C06-0726RSM, 2006 WL 4604854, available at http://projectvote.org/fileadmin/ProjectVote/Legal_Documents/WAC__PI_Decision.pdf.

- *Use of modern matching techniques* (also known in the statistical literature as techniques for record linkage). For example, a model introduced by Fellegi and Sunter[15] formalizes ideas of Howard Newcombe based on likelihood ratios in which it becomes somewhat easier to estimate record linkage parameters (even without training data). Training data is a large representative "truth" set of truly matching and nonmatching pairs of records. In the Fellegi-Sunter model each pair is given a score (or weight). The higher the score, the more likely a pair is to be a match.
- *Use of preprocessing to standardize data elements.* Preprocessing involves breaking fields into components and standardizing components, and a common preprocessing application is the use of address standardization software in which a house-number-and-street-name type of address may be broken into house number, street name, direction words (such as East, Southwest, and so on), and street type (Drive, Avenue) that are given standard spellings or abbreviations. Other methods can facilitate use of name information.[16] Although some of the methods described in this appendix are a good starting point, individual states may need to have specific methods for the types of idiosyncrasies and errors relevant to their individual needs.
- *Accounting for the relative frequency of occurrence of values of strings such as first and last names.* A relatively rare name such as "Zabrinsky" may have more distinguishing power than a common name such as "Smith." The primary purpose of the frequency-based (or value-specific) matching is to downweight pairs having the more commonly occurring values of strings. If one has a large file representing an entire state, then one can compute the frequency-based scores associated with different strings by comparing the entire file against itself. The entire file becomes the surrogate training data. These ideas were introduced by Newcombe and extended by Fellegi and Sunter[17] and by Winkler[18] (Box B.2) in demonstrating how to implement frequency-based matching. In production matching software for the Decennial Censuses (1990 and beyond), Winkler had methods that automatically created the frequency-based weights. The distinguishing power of a particular name may vary considerably by geography. In Minnesota, for example, names such as "Garcia" and "Martinez" were relatively rarer and given more distinguishing power; in California the names are much more common and given less distinguishing power.
- *Accounting for minor typographical error (such as "Smith" versus "Smoth") and having an automatic mechanism for downweighting the matching scores for pairs of strings that do not agree exactly.* Winkler[19] provided such a mechanism (Box B.3), which yields significantly improved matching results in comparison to exact character-by-character matching and often outperforms ad hoc methods of "fuzzy matching." The Jaro-Winkler string comparator is widely used by computer scientists. It is a fast alternative to "edit distance" that measures the

---

[15]Ivan P. Fellegi and Alan B. Sunter, "A Theory for Record Linkage," *Journal of the American Statistical Association* 64(328):1183-1210, December 1969.

[16]See William E. Winkler, "Business Name Parsing and Standardization Software," unpublished report, Statistical Research Division, U.S. Bureau of the Census, Washington, D.C., 1993; and William E. Winkler, "Advanced Methods for Record Linkage," *Proceedings of the Section on Survey Research Methods, American Statistical Association*, pp. 467-472, 1994.

[17]Ivan P. Fellegi and Alan B. Sunter, "A Theory for Record Linkage," *Journal of the American Statistical Association* 64(328):1183-1210, December 1969.

[18]William E. Winkler, "Frequency-based Matching in the Fellegi-Sunter Model of Record Linkage," *Proceedings of the Section on Survey Research Methods, American Statistical Association*, pp. 778-783, 1989.

[19]William E. Winkler, "String Comparator Metrics and Enhanced Decision Rules in the Fellegi-Sunter Model of Record Linkage," *Proceedings of the Section on Survey Research Methods, American Statistical Association*, pp. 354-359, 1990.

APPENDIX B

minimum number of insertions, deletions, and substitutions to get from one string to another and has been extensively vetted using data that are highly similar to DMV and VRD data.

- *Estimation of optimal matching parameters (probabilities in the Fellegi-Sunter model) for classifying pairs as matches or nonmatches.* The probabilities can be computed by comparing an entire state file against itself, using a simple unsupervised learning method such as a properly applied expectation-maximization algorithm,[20] or an alternative method.[21] The optimal parameters have the effect of better separating matches from nonmatches. Although this improves matching, it does not yield estimates of error rates.
- *Providing methods for estimating false match rates.* Estimates of matching rates vary according to the matching scores (or weights). A certain false match rate will be associated with the designation of all pairs above a value U1 as matches. If all pairs above a value U2 are designated as matches where U2 > U1, then the typical result is a lower false match rate and fewer pairs designated as matches. Belin and Rubin[22] and Winkler[23] have given unsupervised learning methods for estimating false match rates in situations for which there are no training data.
- *Providing methods for estimating false nonmatch rates.* Estimates of false nonmatches may partially be accomplished via methods of Winkler,[24] although these techniques may need to be modified if they are to be used on state DMV and VRD files.
- *Use of heuristic search strategies to speed up the matching process when necessary.* Although most changes to VRDs are incremental, an operation involving entire database-to-database comparisons may sometimes be necessary. If two databases each have 5 million records, the number of possible pairs that must be compared is 25×10^{12}, a number that is much too large to search with most computer systems available to states. Heuristic strategies may be needed to reduce significantly the number of pairs that must be compared if the databases involved are large.
- *Use of name rooting equivalency tables that automatically generate common variants of a given name* (for example, Bill, Billy, and Will for William). Such tables greatly reduce the need for multiple manual queries using name variants. Implementation of a name rooting at the SSA would benefit all states that verify voter registration information using the SSA. Notably, name rooting could be used as a component of any intrastate query mechanism as well.

---

[20]William E. Winkler, "Using the EM Algorithm for Weight Computation in the Fellegi-Sunter Model of Record Linkage," *Proceedings of the Section on Survey Research Methods, American Statistical Association*, pp. 667-671, 1988.

[21]William E. Winkler, "String Comparator Metrics and Enhanced Decision Rules in the Fellegi-Sunter Model of Record Linkage," *Proceedings of the Section on Survey Research Methods, American Statistical Association*, pp. 354-359, 1990.

[22]Thomas R. Belin and Donald B. Rubin, "A Method for Calibrating False-Match Rates in Record Linkage," *Journal of the American Statistical Association* 90(430):694-707, 1995.

[23]William E. Winkler, "Automatically Estimation Record Linkage False Match Rates," *Proceedings of the Section on Survey Research Methods, American Statistical Association*, CD-ROM. Also available at http://www.census.gov/srd/papers/pdf/rrs2007-05.pdf.

[24]William E. Winkler, "Matching and Record Linkage," pp. 355-384 in *Business Survey Methods*, Brenda G. Cox et al. (eds.), Wiley, New York, 1995; William E. Winkler, "Approximate String Comparator Search Strategies for Very Large Administrative Lists," *Proceedings of the Section on Survey Research Methods, American Statistical Association*, 2004.

> **BOX B.2**
> **Accounting for Commonly Occurring Names**
>
> The earliest computerized record linkage methods[1] do effectively account for the commonly occurring name plus "chance" date-of-birth phenomenon.
>
> Newcombe's matching classification rule was to use the fields in pairs of records to compute a *matching score*. The idea was that agreement on individual fields was more likely to occur among "truly matching" pairs. Pairs above a certain upper bound were designated as matches; pairs below a certain lower bound were designated as nonmatches; and pairs with in-between scores were held for clerical review (when auxiliary information might be used to fill in missing information or "correct" contradictory information). If the upper bound is raised, then the false positive (false match) rate decreases. If the lower bound is decreased, then the false negative (false nonmatch) rate decreases.
>
> The frequencies (probabilities) used in computing the scores can be estimated a priori using the frequencies in the large administrative lists, recognizing that matters such as "the list of most common names" will change slowly over time (which requires periodic adjustment of that set and the probabilities that those names will occur). Efficiently computed frequencies (conditional probabilities) are optimal in the sense that they can minimize the size of the clerical review region. Further, in many situations such as with voter registration databases or department of motor vehicle files, it is possible to estimate or give reasonable approximations of the error rates even without training data.[2] The earliest matching parameter and error-rate estimation procedures are the easiest to implement and most likely appropriate for VRD files. The most general version of the parameter estimation procedures[3] generalize the iterative scaling procedures of Della Pietra et al.[4]
>
> The frequency-based methods[5] automatically adjust match scores downward for the most frequently occurring first and last names. The effect of the downward adjustment is that pairs of records that are associated with commonly occurring names such as "James Smith" fall into an indeterminate region in which additional information (possibly via clerical review and callbacks) is required to determine matching status. In many situations, it is straightforward to obtain the extra matching information for the indeterminate pairs. Most other (much less commonly occurring names) can be matched effectively because the false positive rate is much less than 0.004 percent when using the combination of name, date of birth, and last four digits of the SSN (that is, typically they uniquely identify).
>
> If the state VRD files can be examined a priori, then for each common first-name-last-name combination, we can find the most frequent dates of birth and lower the matching score of the associated

MATCHING RECORDS WITH UNIQUE IDENTIFIERS

Many of the difficulties described above can be reduced or eliminated through the use of a unique identifier (UID) for every voter, such as a driver's license number. If every voter has a single UID, records for a voter can be matched more simply.

In practice, even UIDs are sometimes improperly keyed in transcribing from a handwritten application or improperly recorded on the application (for example, because digits were transposed or one digit is illegible). If there is an error in the UID, a search could be performed using the name and the date of birth to find all possible UIDs associated with those names and dates to find the UID that is most similar to the one recorded in error—that UID would likely be the "correct" UID for the person in question.

pairs of records. We first lower the matching score for the common name combination and then again for the common dates of birth. To match the pairs with the lowered matching scores, we would need additional corroborating information such as telephone number or middle initial. If driver's license number or the last four digits of the SSN are available, then we can use the string comparators to check whether the pairs of corresponding numbers are almost the same. The corroborating information might vary somewhat in differing states. In particular, some states request e-mail address.

In this situation, it is possible to repeat analogous procedures to raise the worst-case false positive probabilities for certain specific name-date-of-birth combinations while significantly reducing the false match probabilities associated with the same name but different dates-of-birth combinations. This approach has the effect of significantly increasing the number of pairs of records for which match status can effectively be computed.

---

[1] Howard B. Newcombe et al., "Automatic Linkage of Vital Records," *Science* 130(3381):954-959, October 1959; Howard B. Newcombe and James M. Kennedy, "Record Linkage: Making Maximum Use of the Discriminating Power of Identifying Information," *Communications of the Association for Computing Machinery* 5(11):563-566, November 1962.

[2] William E. Winkler, "Comparative Analysis of Record Linkage Decision Rules," *Proceedings of the Section on Survey Research Methods, American Statistical Association*, pp. 829-834, 1992; William E. Winkler, "Improved Decision Rules in the Fellegi-Sunter Model of Record Linkage," *Proceedings of the Section on Survey Research Methods, American Statistical Association*, pp. 274-279, 1993; William E. Winkler, "Automatically Estimation Record Linkage False Match Rates," *Proceedings of the Section on Survey Research Methods, American Statistical Association*, CD-ROM, 2006, also at http://www.census.gov/srd/papers/pdf/rrs2007-05.pdf ; Thomas R. Belin and Donald B. Rubin, "A Method for Calibrating False-Match Rates in Record Linkage," *Journal of the American Statistical Association* 90(430):694-707, 1995.

[3] William E. Winkler, "On Dykstra's Iterative Fitting Procedure," *The Annals of Probability* 18(1):1410-1415, July 1990; William E. Winkler, "Improved Decision Rules in the Fellegi-Sunter Model of Record Linkage," *Proceedings of the Section on Survey Research Methods, American Statistical Association*, pp. 274-279, 1993.

[4] Stephen Della Pietra et al., "Inducing Features of Random Fields," *IEEE Transactions on Pattern Analysis and Machine Intelligence* 19(4):380-393, April 1997.

[5] Howard B. Newcombe et al., "Automatic Linkage of Vital Records," *Science* 130(3381):954-959, October 1959; Howard B. Newcombe and James M. Kennedy, "Record Linkage: Making Maximum Use of the Discriminating Power of Identifying Information," *Communications of the Association for Computing Machinery* 5(11):563-566, November 1962.

A more general strategy would be needed when there is a possibility of typographical error in every field. The matching strategy is to search the entire file and apply suitable proximity metrics that indicate that the UID, first name, last name, and date of birth are sufficiently close to the query record. The feasibility of this strategy depends on the frequency with which invalid UIDs are encountered, because it is not practical to sequentially read every record in the database and perform substantial computation on every record in the file for every query.

The most general strategy involves substantial restructuring of the database to facilitate fast searches. Keys such as first character of first name plus last name plus date of birth, telephone number, or house number plus street name are defined and added to the database to allow fast searches. Using all appropriate fields, only records with proximity scores sufficiently close to the query record are retrieved for review. Definition of the keys and the order in which they are applied requires certain experience and skill.

> **BOX B.3**
> **Blocking and String Comparators**
>
> The two methods for dealing with minor typographical variation are blocking and string comparators. The idea of *blocking* was to search on given characteristics and use remaining information to compute matching scores. For instance, a search might be performed on first initials "J" and "S" and year of birth to retrieve records for which all remaining information is considered to compute a matching score against a record in another database for John Smith. A *string comparator* allows computation of a value for partial agreement for two strings. For instance, a comparison of "John" with "John" might yield a value of 1.0; a comparison of "Johm" with "John" might yield 0.90; and a comparison of "Smith" with "Smeth" might yield 0.94.
>
> The overall matching score can be reduced from the score associated with exact character-by-character agreements on individual fields to account for the partial agreements. Widely used string comparators are edit distance and the Jaro-Winkler string comparator.[1] Code for both methods is widely available on the Internet. Independent verification has consistently shown that the Jaro-Winkler comparator is 10 times as fast as edit distance and returns equally high-quality results with administrative lists of the types that are similar to voter registration databases or department of motor vehicle files.
>
> Other technical approaches to blocking and string comparators can be found in Fienberg et al.[2]
>
> ---
>
> [1] William E. Winkler, "String Comparator Metrics and Enhanced Decision Rules in the Fellegi-Sunter Model of Record Linkage," *Proceedings of the Section on Survey Research Methods, American Statistical Association*, pp. 354-359, 1990; William E. Winkler, "Overview of Record Linkage and Current Research Directions," Statistical Research Division, U.S. Bureau of the Census, Washington, D.C., 2006, available at http://www.census.gov/srd/papers/pdf/rrs2006-02.pdf.
>
> [2] William W. Cohen, Pradeep Ravikumar, and Stephen E. Fienberg, "A Comparison of String Metrics for Matching Names and Addresses," pp. 73-78 in *Proceedings of the Workshop on Information Integration on the Web*, International Joint Conference on Artificial Intelligence, Acapulco, Mexico, August 2003; William W. Cohen, Pradeep Ravikumar, and Stephen E. Fienberg, "A Comparison of String Distance Metrics for Name-Matching Tasks," *Proceedings of the ACM Workshop on Data Cleaning, Record Linkage and Object Identification*, Washington D.C., August 2003.

C

Data Issues

As noted in Appendix B, the quality of data with which matching procedures must work has a significant impact on the rate of false positives and false negatives that result from such procedures.

SOURCES OF VOTER REGISTRATION INFORMATION

The NVRA requires state departments of motor vehicles to incorporate the voter registration application into the application for driver's licenses in a way that does not require the applicant to duplicate any information (except for a second signature). Thus, the DMV is responsible for passing to voter registrars the information needed to register a voter. In most states, the forms are simply sent from DMV offices to the local elections office, where a second manual data entry into the VRD takes place. In a few states, the data from the form is entered into DMV records, and then the proper information is extracted and sent to the registrar electronically (eliminating the need for a second data entry). State DMVs are also required to transmit changes of address received for driver's licenses to the appropriate voter registrar for a change of registration address unless the individual involved indicates otherwise.

The NVRA also requires public assistance and disability service agencies to provide voters with voter registration forms that voters complete manually and then return to the agency or department for delivery to the voter registrar, or to certify in writing that the individual applying for assistance or service has declined the opportunity to register to vote.[1] (However, the committee also recognizes that election officials are not generally in the chain of command for these agencies, a fact that often leads to a certain amount of bureaucratic politics as Agency A seeks to persuade Agency B to help carry out the mission of Agency A.) The availability of registration forms in these many locations increases the opportunities for eligible voters to register, but can also result in duplicate registrations that are sent to election agencies, and if voters themselves fill out the form manually, they can and do make mistakes.

DATA CAPTURE AND QUALITY

Under all procedures used for voter registration in the United States today, the prospective voter must take action to register to vote.[2] Through such action, the voter provides certain pieces of information that eventually wind up in a voter registration database. If this process could be guaranteed to be error-free, many fewer problems of data quality would exist. But unfortunately, this is not the case.

It is useful to distinguish between three categories of error that may be introduced in the journey of these pieces of information from the voter's head to the database. Usually, the voter provides

---

[1] The committee received testimony during its second workshop that many state assistance and service agencies are not following through with this obligation.
[2] Exceptions arise from the fact that some states allow same-day registration and that North Dakota does not require voter registration.

handwritten information on a form. The form is transmitted or carried to the voter registrar, where the data are transcribed from the form into machine-readable form, usually by a data-entry clerk who performs this task manually. Once in machine-readable form, the data may then be processed in some minimal fashion before it is stored permanently in the database. All of these steps can result in some kind of error.

A variety of problems complicate the data capture process. For example, data capture efforts are often compromised by:

- *Illegibility*. The information on most voter registration forms is handwritten, and in many cases, the handwriting is difficult to read, entirely illegible, or misunderstood. This makes the act of entering this information more challenging and increases the potential for errors in voter registration records to be entered in the database.
- *Inaccurate or incomplete voter registration information.* Applicants may fill out the forms inaccurately or incompletely if they misunderstand what information is required. Although applicants make such errors in all venues in which they fill out applications, they are more likely to make errors when the venue is crowded, noisy, and chaotic and when those available to help applicants do not have time or are not knowledgeable enough to answer questions about the applications. These conditions are often met during voter registration drives that take place in locations other than election offices—shopping centers, university campuses, and other locations that attract large crowds. In addition, voter registration drives are frequently staffed by volunteers, some of whom may not have sufficient knowledge of process and procedures in collecting voter information; this may be especially true when volunteers are brought in from out of town.
- *Missing voter registrations.* For example, Jim Dickson of the American Association of People with Disabilities testified to the committee that the volume of voter registration applications received from state social service and disability agencies (a service to potential voters that the NVRA directs these agencies to provide) has dropped significantly since the initial implementation of the law in 1995, although the committee notes that the causality of this drop remains unclear—that is, it is unknown whether this drop reflects failures in the social service agencies to meet their legal obligations; a change in the demographics and/or preferences of those applying for social services; problems in conveying completed applications to voter registrars; or some other reason(s).
- *Repeated (duplicate) registration applications.* An individual may submit multiple voter registration applications "just to be sure," or because s/he may have forgotten that s/he is already registered to vote. Although voter registrars are supposed to have mechanisms in place to screen duplicate registrations, the screening process does not always work smoothly, and sometimes the same individual may be registered more than once.
- *Inconsistencies in submitted information.* In filling out forms, individuals are often unintentionally inconsistent in the information they provide, especially if a period of time has elapsed between multiple form-fillings (either across registrations or between registrations and other activities such as applying for a driver's license or an SSN). An individual may use a nickname in one case and the full legal name in another, or include a middle initial in one and omit it in another. Such inconsistencies may arise because of a lack of clarity in the instructions given to the individual about what specific information to provide or a lack of recall about what s/he entered on a previous occasion. In other cases, the information requested may have changed (names sometimes change upon marriage, for example).
- *Data entry errors.* Typographical errors are made by hitting one key when another was intended. Transposition errors transpose two letters in a field, or even two fields. Even with carefully handwritten registration forms, it is possible that transcription/keying error may

APPENDIX C

TABLE C.1 Illustrative Sources of Error in Names

Source of Error	Name on Voter Registration Form[a]	Name in Database
Typos	Pierce	Peirce or Pearce or Perce or Pierrce
Transliteration	Mohammad	Muhammed
Marriage	Mary Pierce (maiden name Owens)	Mary Owens or Mrs. Martin Pierce
Nickname	Sam Pierce	Samuel Pierce
Transposed field	Bao Lu	Lu Bao
Double names	"Mary Ann" (first) "Pierce" (last)	"Mary" (first) "Ann" (middle) "Pierce" (last)
Hyphenated name	"Mary" (first) "Owens-Pierce" (last)	"Mary" (first") "Owens" (middle) "Pierce" (last)
Punctuation	al-Amin	al Amin
Omitted middle name or initial	John Philip Pierce	John Pierce

[a] Handwriting assumed to be readable.
SOURCE for all rows but the last: Justin Levitt, Wendy R. Weiser, and Ana Muñoz, *Making the List: Database Matching and Verification Processes for Voter Registration,* Brennan Center, New York University, 2006. Reprinted with permission.

approach 5 percent or more in fields such as first name, last name, and date of birth if the data entry clerks lack adequate training and monitoring.[3]

- *Systematic errors stemming from different data representation conventions.* Among the most important are those associated with dates and names.

  —In many countries (including most of Europe), 01/03/2007 means March 1, 2007, whereas in the United States it means January 3, 2007. A naturalized U.S. citizen is perhaps more likely to make such a mistake than an individual raised in the United States.
  —In many Asian nations, the family name is always stated first. Kim Jong-il is a Korean name; the family name is Kim, and the given name is Jong-il. However, it would be easy for an American to recognize Kim as a first name, perhaps as an abbreviation for Kimberly, and Jong-il as a last name.
  —Names normally rendered in an alphabet other than a Roman alphabet may well be spelled inconsistently when transcribed into a Roman alphabet. This problem is of particular concern to those of Russian, Asian, Israeli, and Arabic descent.

These factors generate a wide range of errors. Table C.1 describes a variety of additional error types that may also exist in name fields; Table C.2 describes some possible errors in date-of-birth fields. Voter registrars are left with the problem of managing an environment in which such errors are common.

---

[3] See J.J. Pollock and A. Zamora, "Automatic Spelling Correction in Scientific and Scholary Text," *Communications of the ACM* 27(4):358-368, 1984. In a highly controlled situation, keying error rates were in excess of 2 percent (in keystrokes). A 1-2 percent error rate in keystrokes could easily yield a 5 percent error rate in fields.

TABLE C.2 Illustrative Sources of Error in Dates of Birth

Source of Error	On Voter Registration Form	In Database (Voter, DMV, and/or SSA)
Typos	01/03/05	02/03/05 or 1/00/05 or 1/03/05 or 11/03/05
Transposed field	01/03/05	03/01/05 or 05/01/03
Invented default	01/03/05	01/01/05 (submitted only as January 2005)

SOURCE: Justin Levitt, Wendy R. Weiser, and Ana Muñoz, *Making the List: Database Matching and Verification Processes for Voter Registration,* Brennan Center, New York University, 2006. Reprinted with permission.

Problems with data capture and errors in the voter registration database can have an important effect on the individuals whose data are involved. The voter believes that he or she is properly registered, but the registration may have been rejected as a result of the inaccurate, incomplete, or illegible information on the form, or the voter may not know to bring to the polls on Election Day the additional identification required because of a problem with his or her form. In some cases, the voter may be entirely absent from the voter registration rolls.

Errors in databases will accumulate if action is not taken to correct them promptly. For example, assume that 16 percent of all records in a database reflect at least one change in a field per year. After 3 years, 40 percent of the records will be different. This means that if the database is not updated yearly, 40 percent of the records in the database will be in error.

In addition, it may become more difficult over time to correct errors that occurred at previous time periods in the absence of mechanisms to keep track of individuals uniquely (for example, through driver's license numbers or through secondary systems that keep history)—that is, errors can compound as multiple matches and corrections take place. For instance, if a state VRD file has dates of birth corrected using a semiautomatic procedure that utilizes matching with a state DMV file, then incorrect matching or an erroneous date of birth in the DMV file will induce error in the state VRD file. Subsequent matching against state social services files or SSA files to determine whether an individual is deceased will either fail or possibly induce additional error.

IMPROVING DATA CAPTURE AND QUALITY

A number of approaches are available for improving the quality of data within a VRD. However, all such approaches require certain skills and resources *on a continuing basis.* This last point is important—because of ongoing changes in the population eligible to vote, a continuous effort to maintain data quality in a voter registration database is needed if the database is not to fall into an error-filled state. Inadequate resources for database maintenance will result in greater amounts of error.

The remainder of this section addresses a variety of ways for improving data quality. However, one often-used method for improving data quality is not an option for voter registrars—starting over from scratch. In many cases, databases with errors that accumulate over time eventually become so filled with erroneous data that it is more cost-effective to rebuild the databases from scratch than to try to clean them up. Voter registrars in Kentucky did so in 1973, requiring all voters to re-register. However, "starting from scratch" for a VRD would mean purging everyone from the VRD, and since the NVRA establishes specific criteria for removing voters from registration lists, such an act would be contrary to existing law.

APPENDIX C

Human-assisted Data Cleaning

Many traditional systems for managing administrative lists incorporate procedures that improve data capture and remove some typographical variations. The data-capture procedures are intended to improve the quality (legibility and completeness) of the information on written forms and the subsequent keying of the data-derived information into computer files. In traditional systems, list cleanup is often performed by skilled specialists who can determine name variations or possible missing information in the main administrative files. Using experience and auxiliary information, the specialists might determine that "Johm Smeth" must really be "John Smith." They might determine that the date of birth (in the form MMDDYYYY) "06139182" might have really have been meant to be "06131982."

The intent of the corrections by the specialists was to remove typographical errors in the main administrative list. A cleaned-up list allows more effective searching of large files and effective comparison of pairs of records. For a new record "John Smith" with date of birth "06131982," it is much easier to search for "John Smith" in the corrected administrative list and compare dates of birth or search for "06131982."

Note that some types of typographical error simply cannot be identified using such a technique. Although automated accounting for the presence of typographical errors in a database is often possible, certain "errors" may not in fact be errors. "Bill" is only one character away from "Bull"—and indeed the "i" in Bill may be a mistyped "u," but "Bull" is used as a first name from time to time as well. There are no known ways to handle such "errors" automatically without the availability of tertiary reference data.

In some instances, such as UK national health files or U.S. SSA files, a full-time staff locates, follows up, and corrects for certain types of errors. This effort can significantly reduce the number of individuals who are represented in the lists two or more times. If these cleaned-up lists are used in verifying information associated with other lists, then these other lists are much less likely to induce additional error than are lists that have not undergone intense cleanup.

Voter-assisted Error Correction

New registrants can sometimes be given the opportunity to correct erroneous information. For example, the name and address provided on a registration card may be legible, but the date of birth illegible. If enough legible information is provided, voter registrars can contact the voter to inform him/her of the problem and ask them to resubmit correct information.

In many polling places today, voters can correct registration information—a poll worker notes an error on the registry or on another log, and the election officials can update their registry as part of the postelection canvass. In addition, voters in many states now receive confirmation cards that confirm their registrations; these cards provide the voter with an opportunity to review the information that is part of their registration.

To help minimize keying errors, registrars might ask individuals with access to the relevant facilities to correct their information online through a Web site; security would be provided by a special code or password returned to the individual with the data correction request to ensure that only the proper individual could view or correct the information.

Electronic Transmission of Voter Registration Applications

Important sources of voter registration applications include departments of motor vehicles and social service agencies. Today's processes usually require individuals to register using handwriting on paper forms, a process that is highly subject to error upon data entry. But there is no reason in principle that the information collected by the DMVs and social service agencies (which is almost surely being captured in electronic form for use in DMV or social service agency systems) that is relevant to voter registration could not be transmitted electronically to voter registrars, thereby eliminating errors associated with repeated keying (once for the agency in question and a second time for the VRD). Some states also require that the voter provide a signature for the voter registration record, which is used for verification against pollbooks or ballot return envelopes in the mail-in voting process. An electronic transfer of voter registration forms must therefore accommodate in some way the need for the signature.

Though recommended by the Election Assistance Commission in its *Voluntary Guidance on Implementation of Statewide Voter Registration Lists*,[4] electronic transmission is not required by any present regulation and would entail some nontrivial work to implement on a large scale, such as agreement on the format for transmission and the construction of additional software to permit the exchange of information.

Use of Other Databases (Including Third-party Data)

Yet another way to correct errors in an existing database is to match as many of its records as possible with those in another complete, (nearly) error-free database (or several such databases) and to use these other databases as "truth" for error correction. If there are no such complete high-quality databases available, then the use of other databases can still be useful to triangulate on the correct information, but the error correction process will take a lot more work under these circumstances.

At the same time, the fact that other databases may contain data with fewer errors does not mean that the information they provide should automatically be used to update the voter's registration. Discrepancies between the voter's registration information as represented in the VRD and data in these other databases are indicators of possible errors in the VRD, but in most cases voter registrars are required by law or policy to follow up on such discrepancies by contacting the voter to inquire as to which information is accurate—the voter database or the other database used in the match.

Third-party data, or secondary data, of high quality can be used to reduce ambiguity in record-level matches because they can be used to associate the same identity with a different record using data values based on a different time period or on differences in the values recorded. Sources of such data include telephone books and credit header data (credit records), which can be used to determine or validate middle names, addresses, dates of birth, and so on. Other generally available sources of data sometimes worth consideration include databases of property ownership, magazine subscriptions, and so on. Data aggregators, such as Lexis-Nexis, Choicepoint, and Acxiom, collect data from a variety of disparate sources and sell data on a record-by-record request basis over an Internet connection, although the expense of access to such data may be a significant barrier to their use.

Third-party data vary in quality, with some sources worse than others. In addition, data collected to serve one purpose are sometimes less well suited for another purpose. These issues with quality may affect judgments about the suitability of available third-party data for correcting errors in a VRD.

Note that 94 percent of the parties responding to a 2007 National Association of State Election Directors survey on voter registration practices indicated that they did not use secondary data sources such as phone directories or real-property records to reconstruct a voter's information if information supplied by the voter on a voter registration card was missing or incomplete.[5]

A special source of third-party data for a given state is the VRDs of other states. That is, under most circumstances, an individual can vote in only one jurisdiction. Generally, it violates no law for an individual to be registered to vote in more than one jurisdiction, but the presence of the same person in the VRDs of two states suggests that one of those registrations does not accurately reflect the status of that individual. A number of states have agreed to exchange voter registration data in a couple of ongoing collaborations. Only preliminary data from these collaborations are available at this point, and the

---

[4] Available at http://www.eac.gov/election/docs/statewide_registration_guidelines_072605.pdf/attachment_download/file.
[5] See http://www.surveymonkey.com/sr.aspx?sm=jK8QyNXCIwgdaY4SjASFyN0v4coilbBEvQxDuSyIS4s_3d.

committee looks forward to analyzing more detailed data from these projects in the future, including information on the fields they are matching, the number of potential duplicates on the lists, and the number of actual duplicates they remove from their lists. A start at tracking some efforts at interstate checking of duplicate registrations can be found in the EAC report *Impact of the National Voter Registration Act on Federal Elections 2005-2006*.[6] On page 76 of that report can be found the fact that at least three groups of states have checked for such duplicates at least once: District of Columbia, Virginia, and Maryland; Minnesota, Missouri, Nebraska, Kansas, and Iowa; and Kentucky, South Carolina, and Tennessee.

Improving match accuracy can contribute to improved completeness of a VRD. Match accuracy, whether performed by automated processes or manual review, can be benefited by tertiary, third-party, data. When such external data are carefully harnessed for improved match accuracy, systems can more often resolve ambiguities without human involvement. Reducing the number of exceptions necessitating human review and judgment increases the repeatability of list maintenance.

Such data can be used in two ways. First, such data can be acquired across the entire population and made available for error-correction processes. Second, data can be selectively made available only when they are needed to resolve ambiguities in any putative record-level match—an approach that minimizes privacy concerns because it obtains additional data on individuals only when they are needed.[7]

When using third-party data to enhance matching accuracy, additional logging and accountability requirements must be introduced. Each third-party record requested and received must be retained and retained in its original form until it is no longer needed (for example, until the point that the voter has confirmed any changes that may have resulted from the use of such data). Furthermore, any third-party record used to improve a match should be logged and accounted for similarly. In addition, government matching with third-party datasets raises privacy concerns (such as concerns if credit header data is merged with voter history data, for example).

COLLATERAL ISSUES IN IMPROVING DATA QUALITY

Application of the techniques discussed above is intended to improve the quality of the data in a VRD by making the data more accurate—that is, these techniques allow erroneous data to be changed into correct data. But their success in doing so is not guaranteed—use of the techiques may introduce additional error, or the original data may in fact have been correct. Thus, it may well be advisable to keep the old data as well as the new, but with a flag that indicates that the old data have been corrected. In addition, a policy must be established regarding notification of the voter if a field is changed. The cost of such notification must be weighed against the value of ensuring with high confidence that the updated data are correct.

---

[6] Available at http://www.eac.gov/clearinghouse/docs/the-impact-of-the-national-voter-registration-act-on-federal-elections-2005-2006/attachment_download/file. See also Thad Hall and Michael Alvarez, "The Next Big Election Challenge: Developing Electronic Data Transaction Standards for Election Administration," IBM Center for the Business of Goverment, 2005, available at http://www.vote.caltech.edu/media/documents/AlvarezReport.pdf.

[7] This technique is explained in detail in Paul Rosenzweig and Jeff Jonas, "Correcting False Positives: Redress and the Watch List Conundrum," Legal Memorandum 17, The Heritage Foundation, June 17, 2005, available at http://www.heritage.org/Research/HomelandSecurity/lm17.cfm.

D

Security and Privacy

Voter registration systems are known to be points of risk in election administration systems. Indeed, the ostensible purpose of voter registration is to make the election system more secure against fraud in the first place. When a voter registration system is computer-based, security thus becomes an issue.

Security is the property of a computer system whereby the system does what is required and expected in the face of deliberate attack.[1] For purposes of this report, privacy refers to the protection of the information contained within the VRD against improper access.

As the comments in this appendix indicate, privacy and security issues related to VRDs are not merely technical issues. Indeed, a mix of policy and technology is relevant to their consideration, and these issues are nothing else if not hard to resolve, especially on a limited timescale. It is largely for this reason that the committee does not view these issues as having easy resolution in the short term. Accordingly, the committee will be addressing these issues in its future deliberations, and the final report will include both more substantial analysis and recommendations related to security and privacy.

SECURITY[2]

Although the security of electronic voter registration systems has not been subject to the levels of scrutiny directed at electronic voting systems, the security of VRD systems is nonetheless important. Security of computer systems is usually conceptualized in terms of confidentiality, integrity, and availability:[3]

- *Confidentiality.* A secure system will keep protected information away from those who should not have access to it. Examples of failures that affect the confidentiality of a VRD

---

[1] Reliability in the face of human, machine, or network failure is also an important dimension of system trustworthiness, but this appendix focuses on security against deliberate attack.

[2] There is an extensive body of National Research Council work on computer security issues, beginning with *Computers at Risk: Safe Computing in the Information Age*, 1990, and continuing with *Cryptography's Role in Securing the Information Society*, 1996; *Trust in Cyberspace*, 1999; *Realizing the Potential of C4I: Fundamental Challenges*, 1999; *Making IT Better: Expanding IT Research to Meet Society's Needs*, 2000; *Cybersecurity Today and Tomorrow: Pay Now or Pay Later*, 2002; *Software for Dependable Systems: Sufficient Evidence?*, 2007; and *Toward a Safer and More Secure Cyberspace*, 2007, all published by the National Academy [Academies] Press, Washington, D.C. In addition, an extensive discussion of security and privacy issues specifically with reference to voter registration databases is contained in U.S. Public Policy Committee of the Association for Computing Machinery, *Statewide Databases of Registered Voters: Study of Accuracy, Privacy, Usability, Security, and Reliability Issues*, 2006, available at http://usacm.acm.org/usacm/PDF/VRD_report.pdf. Excerpts from the executive summary of this report relevant to privacy and security are provided in Box D.1.

[3] See for example, NRC, *Toward a Safer and More Secure Cyberspace*, The National Academies Press, Washington, D.C., 2007.

include an unauthorized party obtaining voter information on a large scale or a spouse abuser obtaining the address of his/her spouse from a VRD even if such information is supposed to be protected.
- *Integrity.* A secure system produces the same results or information whether or not the system has been attacked. When integrity is violated, the system may continue to operate, but under some circumstances of operation it does not provide accurate results or information that one would normally expect. An example of a failure that affects the integrity of a VRD is an unauthorized change in a VRD that could force an individual to show identification at the polls when in fact there is no such requirement for that individual to do so.
- *Availability.* A secure system is available for normal use even in the face of an attack. An example of a failure in availability might be a system that is clogged with so much bad data that the system no longer operates reliably (for example, a flood of bogus paper voter registration applications that overwhelms the data-entry staff in a particularly critical jurisdiction).

A number of security breaches of VRDs have been reported.[4] For example, on October 23, 2006, an official from the not-for-profit Illinois Ballot Integrity Project reported that his organization had used the Chicago voter database remotely to compromise the names, SSNs, and dates of birth of 1.35 million residents. According to a spokesman for the Chicago Election Board, the problem arose because the city's database allowing voters to locate their voting precinct once asked voters for detailed information such as Social Security numbers, and even though the Web site was updated to require only names and addresses to make a query, the links to the Social Security numbers and the dates of birth were never eliminated.[5]

Developing secure systems (where "system" is intended to include the human and organizational aspects of a system as well as the technology) is a challenging task, and much has been written about such matters. But it is essential to consider three fundamental points about security.

First, good security practices require thinking about building security in from the start. Good system specifications inform analysts of what is "required and expected" behavior. Good software engineering enables the system to be implemented in a way that conforms to the system specification. Formal verification methods and other analysis tools may be helpful in showing that implementations faithfully conform to certain aspects of their specifications.

Second, security threats can arise even in systems that are not connected to the Internet. Although Internet connections are often an important source of vulnerability, they are most assuredly not the only source. The recent history of computer security is replete with examples of security compromises that had nothing to do with the Internet, such as data on stolen laptops, attacks from insiders abusing their privileges, and "social engineering" attacks involving humans posing as other humans, often over the telephone, in order to learn credentials such as passwords that can enable them to access systems and files they should not be able to access.

For example, video surveillance cameras caught two intruders in Mississippi on June 23, 2006, stealing hard drives from 18 computers. Data files contained names, addresses, and SSNs of current and former city employees and registered voters as well as bank account information for employees paid through direct deposit and water system customers who paid bills electronically.[6]

Third, any realistic assessment of a system's security involves actual testing of the system's security by an adversary who is motivated to compromise it. Although testing cannot, and does not,

---

[4] See http://www.privacyrights.org/ar/ChronDataBreaches.htm. This site contains descriptions of a number of data breaches involving actual VRDs, and a number of others of potential relevance to VRDs.
[5] See http://abcnews.go.com/Politics/story?id=2601085; http://www.electiondefensealliance.org/chicago_voter_registration_database_wide_open.
[6] See http://www.privacyrights.org/ar/ChronDataBreaches.htm.

> # BOX D.1
> ## Excerpts from a 2006 Study of Voter Registration Databases Relevant to Privacy and Security
>
> The following material is reprinted from the executive summary and the main text of *Statewide Databases of Registered Voters: Study of Accuracy, Privacy, Usability, Security, and Reliability Issues,* a 2006 report by the U.S. Public Policy Committee of the Association for Computing Machinery.
>
> 2. Accountability should be apparent throughout each VRD.
>
> It should be clear who is proposing, making, or approving changes to the data, the system, or its policies. Security policies are an important tool for ensuring accountability. For example, access control policies can be structured to restrict actions of certain groups or individual users of the system. Further, users' actions can be logged using audit trails (discussed below). Accountability also should extend to external uses of VRD data. For example, state and local officials should require recipients of data from VRDs to sign use agreements consistent with the government's official policies and procedures.
>
> 3. Audit trails should be employed throughout the VRD.
>
> VRDs that can be independently verified, checked, and proven to be fair will increase voter confidence and help avoid litigation. Audit trails are important for independent verification, which, in turn, makes the system more transparent and provides a mechanism for accountability. They should include records of data changes, configuration changes, security policy changes, and database design changes. The trails may be independent records for each part of the VRD, but they should include both who made the change and who approved the change.
>
> 4. Privacy values should be a fundamental part of the VRD, not an afterthought.
>
> Privacy policies for voter registration activities should be based on Fair Information Practices (FIPs), which are a set of principles for addressing concerns about information privacy. FIPs typically address collection limitation, data quality, purpose specification, use limitation, security safeguards, openness, individual participation, and accountability. There are many ways to implement good privacy policies. For example, we recommend that government both limit

necessarily reveal all security problems (and does nothing by itself to eliminate such problems), testing can often identify some remaining failures.

PRIVACY

Some of the information in VRDs is, by law, public information, although the specifics of which data items can be regarded as public information vary from state to state. In addition, states often limit the purposes for which such information may be used. Nevertheless, the electronic availability of such information raises concerns about the privacy of that information, because electronic access greatly increases the ease with which it can be made available to anyone, including those who might abuse it.

One of the thorniest issues regarding privacy is the tension it sometimes poses with transparency. In its starkest terms, maintaining privacy involves withholding certain information associated with individuals from public view, while transparency involves the maximum disclosure of information, even if such information is associated with individuals.

collection to only the data required for proper registration and explain why each piece of personal information is necessary. Further, privacy policies should be published and widely distributed, and the public should be given an opportunity to comment on any changes. . . .

6. Election officials should rigorously test the usability, security and reliability of VRDs while they are being designed and while they are in use.

Testing is a critical tool that can reveal that "real-world" poll workers find interfaces confusing and unusable, expose security flaws in the system, or that the system is likely to fail under the stress of Election Day. All of these issues, if caught before they are problems through testing will reduce voter fraud and the disenfranchisement of legitimate voters. . . .

Security Against Technical Attacks

. . . [M]echanisms should be deployed to detect any penetration of system defenses, as well as any insider misuse. For example, application-specific intrusion detection systems could be used to monitor the number of updates to the VRD. Any large spike in activity, whether by an authorized user or in the aggregate, might warrant human attention. In addition, officials could consider contracting with a third-party network security monitoring service to detect network intrusions and attempted attacks on the system. . . .

. . . Officials should consider including an independent security review and publication of the software as part of the acceptance testing for the system. Claims that the security of the system will be endangered by such a review should be treated with extreme skepticism or rejected outright. . . .

SOURCE: U.S. Public Policy Committee of the Association for Computing Machinery, *Statewide Databases of Registered Voters: Study of Accuracy, Privacy, Usability, Security, and Reliability Issues,* 2006, available at http://usacm.acm.org/usacm/PDF/VRD_report.pdf. (c) 2006 ACM. Excerpted with permission. ISBN: 1-59593-344-1. Permission to make digital or hard copies of portions of this work for personal or classroom use is granted without fee provided that copies are not made or distributed for profit or commercial advantage and that copies bear this notice and the full citation on the first page. To copy otherwise, to republish, to post on servers or to redistribute to lists, requires prior specific permission and/or a fee. Request permission from permissions@acm.org.

As an illustration of how these tensions play out, consider a proposition regarding the public disclosure of the reason(s) for removing specific individuals from voter registration lists. On one hand, the removal of a voter from a VRD is often associated with a stigmatizing condition, such as being a felon or being declared mentally incompetent. Those mistakenly removed from a VRD may experience adverse consequences from such association, and even if the removal is correctly performed, those individuals are still arguably entitled to some measure of privacy. Thus, a person balancing the scales in favor of privacy would argue that the reasons for removing individuals from the VRD should be kept confidential, as they are in some states already.

On the other hand, advocates of greater transparency argue that removals from a VRD should be subject to public oversight in the same way that additions are. They point out that convictions and even arrest records are generally public, and thus argue that not disclosing reasons for removal from a VRD does not really protect the privacy of these individuals anyway. At the same time, they argue that associating reasons for removal with specific individuals is critical to determining the qualification of voters—and that statistical tabulations alone would not provide the detail needed to investigate individual errors that might indicate systemic problems.

The committee noted significant value without much negative impact on privacy in statistical tabulations of the reasons for voters being dropped from a VRD and publication of such tabulations, as well as in personal and private notification of individual voters of the reason(s) for being dropped. But the different points of view described above were reflected in the committee, and thus the committee takes no position on the desirability or undesirability of the above proposition. The committee might address this point in its final report.

Other privacy advocates have raised concerns about the widespread availability of complete voter registration information in the context of the physical security of battered men or women. Such individuals have good reason to keep their addresses private, and might be apprehensive with good reason about the availability of their addresses to their batterers. A second concern relates to abuse of lists of validated addresses for commercial marketing purposes—many citizens would be upset to know that the information they provided to exercise their right to vote in a democracy is also being used for commercial purposes. Addressing such issues properly belongs to state policy makers, who can develop (and sometimes have developed) regulation and law to protect citizen interests—for example, some states only allow political parties to obtain voter registration lists.

A second set of privacy issues arises from matching and linking records. For example, voter registration lists may be matched against a list of convicted felons. If a list of voters removed from the VRD is made public, those removed from the list improperly or removed for other reasons (that is, all nonfelons removed from the list) may be tainted by association in the public eye. Similarly, if a voter registration list is made public that indicates the source of an individual application, those who registered to vote at public assistance agencies might regard their privacy rights as having been violated. Although overt public disclosure would violate the NVRA, accidental disclosure through a security breach might have a similar result. This could in turn reduce the likelihood that people will seek out public assistance if seeking it will automatically place that information in a voter registration record that is publicly accessible. Alternatively, where registration is not automatic, it may reduce the number of individuals who take advantage of the ease of registering at the public assistance agency and thereby undercut the goal of the program.

A third set of privacy issues arises from insider access to the VRD. Insiders such as election officials could be expected to have access to the full set of information associated with any individual record, and possibly to some of the information in matched records existing in other databases. Although most election officials are trustworthy in this regard, a few might seek to use this access—improperly—for personal benefit or gain, and security measures (such as tamper-proof audit logs) are needed to prevent or deter such inappropriate insider access.

E

Workshop Agendas

WORKSHOP OF AUGUST 6, 2007, WASHINGTON, D.C.

10:30–10:45 a.m. **Welcome to the Workshop**
Sharon Priest and Olene Walker, Committee and Workshop Co-chairs

10:45–12:00 p.m. **Panel I   Overview of the Issues**

What are key voter registration issues, and how do they affect the establishment of statewide voter registration databases as mandated by HAVA?
Moderator: *Sharon Priest/Olene Walker*

Panelists:
Gracia M. Hillman, Commissioner, U.S. Election Assistance Commission
Caroline C. Hunter, Commissioner, U.S. Election Assistance Commission
Leonard M. Shambon, formerly with Wilmer Cutler Pickering Hale and Dorr
Robert A. Pastor, Executive Director, Carter-Baker Commission and Director of the Center for Democracy and Election Management, American University

Q&A with presenters

12:00–12:45 Lunch Available
Continue discussion from first panel session and prepare for afternoon sessions

12:45–2:15 **Panel II   Status of Voter Registration Database Efforts**

What are the different types of and approaches to voter registration systems? What are the benefits and tradeoffs? Do you build it on your own or do you contract it out? What are some upcoming challenges that will need to be addressed in the near term (1-2 years) and in the longer term (5+ years)?
Moderator: *Bruce McPherson*

Panelists:
Deborah Markowitz, Secretary of State, Vermont, and Immediate Past President of the National Association of Secretaries of State
Brad Bryant, President, National Association of State Election Directors and Deputy Assistant for Elections, Kansas
Linda Lindberg, General Registrar, Arlington County, Virginia

Q&A with presenters

2:15–2:30	Break
2:30	*Web Cast Begins*
2:30–2:35	**Welcome and Brief Overview for Web Cast Audience** *Sharon Priest and Olene Walker, Committee and Workshop Co-chairs*
2:35–4:00	**Panel III Record Matching: Technical/Operational Issues and Problems** What types of technical problems can occur in record linking? What is the impact on data quality? What type of data cleaning is required? What are potential solutions to these problems? Moderator: *William Winkler* Panelists: Gio Wiederhold, Professor (Emeritus), Computer Science, Medicine, and Electrical Engineering, Stanford University William Cohen, Associate Research Professor, Machine Learning Department, Carnegie Mellon University Michael Franklin, Professor, Electrical Engineering and Computer Sciences, University of California, Berkeley Respondents: James Willis, Principal, Banyan Social Technology, and Former Director, eGovernment for Rhode Island Frank Olken, Computer Scientist, Lawrence Berkeley National Laboratory Q&A with presenters
4:00–5:30	**Panel IV Interoperability and Database Operations in Other Domains** What kinds of problems or issues exist in non-election domains (i.e., government and nongovernmental settings), including technical and organization dimensions? What is the range of possible solutions? Moderator: *Paula Hawthorn* Panelists: John Glaser, Vice President and Chief Information Officer, Partners Healthcare System Dan Schutzer, Executive Director, Financial Services Technology Consortium Vivek Narasayya, Senior Researcher, Data Management, Exploration and Mining Group, Microsoft Research Ken Orr, Founder, Ken Orr Institute (participating by phone and Web conference) Q&A with presenters
5:30	Adjourn
5:30–6:30 p.m.	Open Reception

APPENDIX E

WORKSHOP OF NOVEMBER 29-30, 2007, WASHINGTON, D.C.

Thursday, November 29, 2007

8:30–8:40 a.m. **Welcome to the Workshop**
Olene Walker, Committee and Workshop Co-chair

8:40–10:15 **Panel I Data Providers Issues and Challenges**
Moderator: *William Winkler*

Panelists:
Peter Monaghan, Director, Information Exchange and Computer Matching, Social Security Administration
William L. Farrell, Director, Office of Systems Security Operations Management, Social Security Administration
Walter A. Jackson III, Senior Systems Analyst, Systems Analysis Division, American Association of Motor Vehicle Administrators
James Wilson, Program Manager, Address Technology, U.S. Postal Service
Garland Land, Executive Director, National Association for Public Health Statistics and Information Systems

Q&A with presenters

10:15–10:45 Break

10:45–11:45 **Panel I Data Providers Issues and Challenges—continued**
Moderator: *Paula Hawthorn*

Respondents:
Kimball Brace, President, Election Data Services (remote participation)
Clark Bensen, Principal Consultant, Polidata
Keith Cunningham, Director of the Board of Elections for Allen County, Ohio

Q&A with presenters

11:45–1:00 p.m. Lunch Available
Continue discussion from morning sessions and prepare for afternoon panels

1:00–3:00 **Panel II IT Operations—State and Local**
Moderator: *John Lindback*

Panelists:
Ray Palmer, Information Technology Manager, Office of the Governor, Utah
Mike Stewart, Chief Information Officer, Office of the Secretary of State, Kansas
Paul Miller, Technical Services Manager, Elections Division, Office of Secretary of State, Washington
Shane Hamlin, Assistant Director of Elections, Office of Secretary of State, Washington

Q&A with presenters

3:00–3:15	Break
3:15–4:45	**Panel III Impact of Technical Implementation on Policy** Moderator: *Olene Walker* Panelists: *Wendy R. Weiser, Deputy Director, Brennan Center for Justice at NYU School of Law* *James C. Dickson, Vice President of Government Affairs, American Association of People with Disabilities* *Melanie L. Campbell, Executive Director, National Coalition on Black Civic Participation* *Lloyd Leonard, Senior Director for Advocacy, League of Women Voters* Q&A with presenters
4:45–5:45	**Panel III Impact of Technical Implementation on Policy—continued** Moderator: *Michael Alvarez* Panelists: *Vincent Keenan, Executive Director, Publius* *Michael P. McDonald, Associate Professor, George Mason University and Non-Resident Senior Fellow, Brookings Institution* *Chris Thomas, Director, Bureau of Elections, Michigan Department of State* *Ernie Hawkins, CERA, Chair of Election Center Board of Directors, California* Q&A with presenters
5:45–6:15 p.m.	Reception—Rotunda

Friday, November 30, 2007

8:30–8:35 a.m.	**Welcome and Overview** *Olene Walker, Committee and Workshop Co-chair*
8:35–10:00	**Panel IV Security and Privacy Issues** Moderator: *Jeff Jonas* Panelists: *Peter G. Neumann, SRI International Computer Science Laboratory* *Glenn Newkirk, President, InfoSENTRY Services Inc. (remote participation)* *James J. Horning, Chief Scientist, Information Systems Security Operation, SPARTA Inc.* *Bradley A. Malin, Assistant Professor, Department of Biomedical Informatics, Vanderbilt University* Q&A with presenters
10:00–10:30	Break

10:30–11:15 **Panel V IT Operations—Vendors**
Moderator: *John Lindback*

Panelists:
Thomas H. Ferguson, Director, Saber Corporation
Neil McClure, Chief Technology Officer, Hart InterCivic

11:15 a.m.   Workshop Adjourns

F

Biographical Information

COMMITTEE MEMBERS

Frances Ulmer, *Co-chair*, is the interim chancellor of the University of Alaska, Anchorage, bringing to this position 30 years of experience in public policy in Alaska. Previously, she was a fellow at the Institute of Politics at Harvard University's Kennedy School of Government and a Distinguished Visiting Professor of Public Policy at the Institute of Social and Economic Research. In the early 1980s, she was the mayor of Juneau, then became a member of the Alaska House of Representatives (1986-1994), and in 1994 became the first female lieutenant governor of Alaska. In that year, she was appointed to the North Pacific Anadromous Fish Commission by President Bill Clinton and served on this international board for 11 years. She has participated in numerous panels, task forces, commissions, and forums as a speaker, moderator, and panelist to address the intersection of science, economics, politics, and policy. She currently serves on the Board of Trustees of the National Parks Conservation Association, the Advisory Board of the Union of Concerned Scientists, and the Alaska Nature Conservancy Board. At the national level, Ms. Ulmer has served as a member of the above-mentioned North Pacific Anadromous Fish Commission, the Federal Communications Commission's State and Local Advisory Committee, and the Federal Elections Commissions Committee. She has a B.A. in political science and economics and a law degree from the University of Wisconsin.

Olene Walker, *Co-chair*, was the first woman governor of the state of Utah. Before being appointed as governor, she served as the first woman lieutenant governor of Utah. During her time in office, Dr. Walker spearheaded many important initiatives, including education programs, budget security measures, health care reform, and workforce development. She also worked to implement the federal "motor voter" legislation in Utah and oversaw the plan to bring Utah into compliance with the Help America Vote Act (HAVA). She has chaired the National Conference of Lieutenant Governors and is a past president of the National Association of Secretaries of State. She was the first lieutenant governor ever to serve as the president of that organization. Dr. Walker received her bachelor's, master's, and doctoral degrees from Brigham Young University, Stanford University, and the University of Utah, respectively.

Rakesh Agrawal, NAE, is a Microsoft Technical Fellow at the newly founded Search Labs. His areas of expertise are in developing fundamental data mining concepts and technologies and pioneering key concepts in data privacy, including Hippocratic Database, Sovereign Information Sharing, and Privacy-Preserving Data Mining. He is the recipient of the ACM-SIGKDD First Innovation Award, ACM-SIGMOD Edgar F. Codd Innovations Award, ACM-SIGMOD Test of Time Award, VLDB 10-Year Most Influential Paper Award, and the Computerworld First Horizon Award. He is a member of the National Academy of Engineering, a fellow of the Association for Computing Machinery, and a fellow of IEEE. Scientific American named him to the list of 50 top scientists and technologists in 2003. Prior to joining Microsoft in March 2006, Dr. Agrawal was an IBM fellow and led the Quest group at the IBM Almaden Research Center. Earlier, he was with the Bell Laboratories, Murray Hill, from 1983 to 1989. He also worked for 3 years at India's premier company, the Bharat Heavy Electricals Ltd. He received M.S. and Ph.D. degrees in computer science from the University of Wisconsin-Madison in 1983. He also holds a

APPENDIX F

B.E. degree in electronics and communication engineering from IIT-Roorkee, as well as a 2-year postgraduate diploma in industrial engineering from the National Institute of Industrial Engineering (NITIE), Bombay.

R. Michael Alvarez is a professor of political science at the California Institute of Technology (CalTech). His research interests have been in the areas of elections and electoral behavior, survey methodology, statistics and political methodology, and more recently, election administration. Professor Alvarez is currently the co-director of the Caltech/MIT Voting Technology Project and recently co-authored a book published by the Brookings Institution Press, *Point, Click and Vote: The Future of Internet Voting*. Professor Alvarez received his Ph.D. and M.A. degrees in political science from Duke University and his B.A., magna cum laude, in political science from Carleton College.

Charlotte Cleary, retired, was general registrar of Arlington for 19 years. As such, she was responsible for planning, organizing, and directing voter registration and elections. After she retired, she continued working in the election field on a temporary basis. She has served as a member of the writing and research team for the Poll Worker Institute grant on poll worker recruitment, training, and retention, for the Election Assistance Commission. In 2004 she served on the Virginia State Board of elections evaluation committee to review requests for proposals for the new statewide election system. She was a certified professional general registrar in Virginia under the Weldon Cooper Center from 1994 through 2000. She has been a member of the Federal Election Commission Advisory Panel from 1998 through 2003, the Election Center from 1990 through 2003, and the Constitution Project Forum on Election Reform from 2001 to 2003. She received a B.A. in English from American University, in Washington, D.C.

Gary W. Cox, NAS, is a professor of political science at the University of California, San Diego. In addition to numerous articles in the areas of legislative and electoral politics, Professor Cox is author of *The Efficient Secret* (winner of the Samuel H. Beer dissertation prize in 1983 and of the 2003 George H. Hallett Award), coauthor of *Legislative Leviathan* (winner of the Richard F. Fenno Prize in 1993), author of *Making Votes Count* (winner of the Woodrow Wilson Foundation Award, the Luebbert Prize, and the Best Book in Political Economy Award in 1998); and coauthor of *Elbridge Gerry's Salamander: The Electoral Consequences of the Reapportionment Revolution*. His latest book, *Setting the Agenda*, was published in 2005. A former Guggenheim Fellow, Professor Cox was elected to the American Academy of Arts and Sciences in 1996 and to the National Academy of Sciences in 2005. He received a Ph.D. from the California Institute of Technology in 1983.

Paula Hawthorn, retired, serves as a consultant and continues her involvement with the University of California, Berkeley. She received her Ph.D. in electrical engineering and computer science from the University of California in 1979. Her thesis topic was on the performance of database systems. She has spent much of her career as a manager of database development, including vice-president of Software Development for start-ups such as Britton Lee and Illustra, and both management and individual contributor positions at Hewlett-Packard (working on database performance issues) and Lawrence Berkeley National Laboratory.

Sarah Ball Johnson currently serves as the executive director of the Commonwealth of Kentucky's State Board of Elections. She has 12 years of experience in election administration on the state level. She has a bachelor of arts degree in business administration from Transylvania University and a master of public administration degree, specializing in state and local government, from the University of Kentucky. She participated in four international election observation trips, to Slovakia, Kosovo, Macedonia, and Nigeria. A member of the National Association of State Election Directors, she serves as the southern region representative on the board of the association and also serves on the Election Assistance Commission

Standards Board. She was elected by her peers to the Executive Committee of the Standards Board and serves as chair of that committee. She is a member of the Election Center.

Jeff Jonas is a distinguished engineer and chief scientist of Entity Analytic Solutions at IBM. He is responsible for shaping the overall technical strategy of next-generation identity analytics and the use of this new capability in the overall IBM technology strategy. The IBM Entity Analytic Solutions group was formed based on technologies he developed as the founder and chief scientist of Systems Research & Development (SRD). SRD was acquired by IBM in January 2005. He applies his real-world experience in software design and development to drive technology innovations while delivering higher levels of privacy and civil liberties protections. He is a member of the Markle Foundation Task Force on National Security in the Information Age and actively contributes on issues of privacy, technology, and homeland security to leading national think tanks, privacy advocacy groups, and policy research organizations, including the Center for Democracy and Technology, Heritage Foundation, Center for Strategic and International Studies, and the Office of the Secretary of Defense Highlands Forum.

John Lindback is director of elections for the state of Oregon, a position he has held since March 2001. His duties include enforcing laws governing the conduct of elections in Oregon, enforcing Oregon's campaign finance laws, administering the state's initiative and referendum process, and publishing state voters' pamphlets. Previously, he worked for 6 years as chief of staff for the lieutenant governor of Alaska, a job that included administrative oversight of Alaska's statewide election system. After earning a journalism degree from the University of Arizona in 1976, Mr. Lindback reported on government for newspapers for 12 years. He has worked in the public sector since 1988 as a budget analyst, legislative finance aide, public information officer, chief of staff to a lieutenant governor, and now state elections director. He is secretary of the National Association of State Elections Directors. He was also elected to the Executive Board of the Elections Assistance Commission's national Standards Advisory Board, a group composed of 110 elections officials from across the nation.

Bruce McPherson was the 30th California secretary of state. The first 26 years of his career he worked in the newsroom of the family-owned *Santa Cruz Sentinel*, serving as sports editor, news reporter, editor-editorial writer, and city editor. During this time he served on, and was president of, numerous community organizations. In his 11 years in the California legislature, he focused his attention on education, environmental protection, and public safety. In the aftermath of the resignation in early 2005 of California's secretary of state, he was nominated by Governor Arnold Schwarzenegger to be secretary of state. Mr. McPherson was confirmed unanimously in both the Senate and the Assembly. While in office, he updated the information technology required to meet election laws, and he oversaw three statewide elections and two special elections. Mr. McPherson graduated from Cal Poly–San Luis Obispo with a B.S. degree in journalism in 1965. He subsequently was given an honorary degree in humane letters from Cal Poly–San Luis Obispo in 2005.

Wendy Noren is county clerk of Boone County, Missouri, a position she has held since 1982, and she managed the election division of the office for 4 years prior to that. Ms. Noren is responsible for keeping records of the orders, rules, and proceedings of the County Commission. In addition, she is responsible for inspecting and reviewing all voter precinct boundaries within the county and conducting elections. Throughout this period, she has served as a programmer for all of the voter registration functions. Over the past 25 years, she has been one of the first to implement emerging technology for the county's voter registration system—often years before most jurisdictions. As both the programmer and user, she has a unique perspective on the critical components of a voter registration system. Other administrative responsibilities of the clerk include maintaining payroll files, administering employee benefits, administering the records management budget, and procuring adequate insurance and bonding for the county's assets and elected officials.

APPENDIX F

William Winkler is a principal researcher with the U.S. Census Bureau. He is a fellow of the American Statistical Association. He has published more than 130 papers and has developed eight (and counting) generalized computer systems for record linkage, edit/imputation, multipurpose and multiway sampling, text classification, and masking for public-use microdata. Dr. Winkler holds a Ph.D. in probability theory from Ohio State University.

Rebecca N. Wright is an associate professor of computer science at Rutgers University. She is also deputy director of the DIMACS Center for Discrete Mathematics and Theoretical Computer Science. Prior to that, she was a professor of computer science at Stevens Institute of Technology and a researcher in the Secure Systems Research Department at AT&T Labs and AT&T Bell Labs. Her research spans the area of information security, including cryptography, privacy, foundations of computer security, and fault-tolerant distributed computing. Professor Wright serves as an editor of the Journal of Computer Security and the International Journal of Information and Computer Security, and was a member of the board of directors of the International Association for Cryptologic Research from 2001 to 2005. She was a co-author on a study, "Statewide Databases of Registered Voters: Study of Accuracy, Privacy, Usability, Security, and Reliability Issues," commissioned by USACM. She was an invited speaker in the National Academy of Engineering's 2007 U.S. Frontiers of Engineering Symposium. She received a Ph.D. in Computer Science from Yale University in 1994 and a B.A. from Columbia University in 1988.

CSTB STAFF

Herbert S. Lin is chief scientist, CSTB at the Computer Science and Telecommunications Board, National Research Council of the National Academies, where he has been the study director for major projects on public policy and information technology. These studies include a 1996 study on national cryptography policy (*Cryptography's Role in Securing the Information Society*), a 1991 study on the future of computer science (*Computing the Future*), a 1999 study of Defense Department systems for command, control, communications, computing, and intelligence (*Realizing the Potential of C4I: Fundamental Challenges*), a 2000 study on workforce issues in high-technology (*Building a Workforce for the Information Economy*), a 2002 study on protecting kids from Internet pornography and sexual exploitation (*Youth, Pornography, and the Internet*), a 2004 study on aspects of the FBI's information technology modernization program (*A Review of the FBI's Trilogy IT Modernization Program*), a 2005 study on electronic voting (*Asking the Right Questions About Electronic Voting*), and a 2005 study on computational biology (*Catalyzing Inquiry at the Interface of Computing and Biology*). Prior to his NRC service, he was a professional staff member and staff scientist for the House Armed Services Committee (1986-1990), where his portfolio included defense policy and arms control issues. He received his doctorate in physics from MIT.

Kristen R. Batch is an associate program officer for the Computer Science and Telecommunications Board of the National Academies. She is currently involved with projects focusing on the interoperability of voter registration databases, the policy and ethical implications of offensive information warfare, and the information technology R&D ecosystem. Since joining CSTB in 2002, she has worked on studies that produced *Toward a Safer and More Secure Cyberspace, Engaging Privacy and Information Technology in a Digital Age, Asking the Right Questions About Electronic Voting, Signposts in Cyberspace: The Domain Name System and Internet Navigation, A Review of the FBI's Trilogy Information Technology Modernization Program*, and *The Internet Under Crisis Conditions: Learning from September 11*. While pursuing an M.A. in international communications from American University, she interned at the National Telecommunications and Information Administration, in the Office of International Affairs, and at the Center for Strategic and International Studies, in the Technology and Public Policy Program. She also received a B.A. from Carnegie Mellon University in literary and cultural studies and Spanish, and she received two travel grants to conduct independent research in Spain.

Morgan R. Motto, senior program assistant, has been with CSTB since December 2007 supporting several projects, including the Wireless Technology Prospects and Policy and Assessing the Impacts of Changes in the Information Technology Research and Development Ecosystem projects. Previously, she worked with the Board on Environmental Studies and Toxicology (BEST) on the reports *Human Biomonitoring for Environmental Chemicals, Sediment Dredging at Superfund Megasites, Applications of Toxicogenomic Technologies to Predictive Toxicology and Risk Assessment, Evaluating Research Efficiency in the U.S. Environmental Protection Agency, Respiratory Disease Research at NIOSH, Review of the Federal Strategy to Address Environmental, Health, and Safety Research Needs for Engineered Nanoscale Materials,* and *Improving Risk Analysis Approaches Used by the US EPA.* Prior to coming to the NRC, Ms. Motto worked as a project manager for international affairs and technology at the U.S. Pan Asian American Chamber of Commerce. She earned a B.A. in international affairs and East Asian studies from the Elliott School of International Affairs at the George Washington University.